## What People Are Saying About *ROR*

*ROR: Return on Relationships* nails it. This book clearly defines "authentic leadership" adding that it needs to be heart centered. And now, more than ever, as we move through these perilous times with the pandemic and social justice issues, employees need to feel that their leaders care and are transparent. Roxanne not only lays out the five elements of authentic heart leadership but gives practical advice about how to achieve it. As an EAP and Organizational Consulting professional, my company has seen organizations who demonstrate this style of leadership become successful as they create a culture of authenticity. A must read for any leader interested in leading in a crisis or in good times.

Bernie Dyme, LCSW, President and CEO, Perspectives LTD.,
Forbes Business Council Member

In a world that seems to constantly demand a "facade," *Return on Relationships* is indeed a manual for building and sustaining authentic relationships across every sphere of human interaction. Roxanne Derhodge beautifully explores a 360° excavation of our relationships and interactions in an easy-to-read, thought-provoking and fascinating manner. I thoroughly commend how this book uncovers layers of authentic reflections and prompts actions for self-awareness, authenticity and sustainable relationship building. *Return on Relationships* is definitely a mandatory read for any progressive individual, especially leaders who want to become exceptional.

Kemi Ogunkoya, Chief Executive Officer, Rellies Works
International, Forbes Business Council Member

Roxanne Derhodge confidently tackles the subject of authentic leadership – how people obtain it, the role of emotional intelligence and how it contributes to extraordinary success. In a clear and compelling manner, she explains how leaders can create their own authentic leadership style based on practical, actionable insight. Roxanne outlines a simple and straightforward methodology that clarifies an often-confusing topic.

If you are a leader, this is a must-read about the most important aspects of developing authentic leadership. Roxanne walks you through a smart, concise and yet thorough review of how to develop authentic leadership skills through aspects of emotional intelligence.

Linda Fisk, CEO and Founder, LeadHERship Global,
Forbes Business Council Member

Shifting the leadership conversation from "how to" to "why do," Roxanne Derhodge takes you on a practical and reflective journey. *Return on Relationships* honours that, in the fast-paced, ever-changing and noisy business context of today, it *is* possible for leaders to find joy, focus and success in their everyday work. The authentic leadership model presented here helps leaders to retain great people, drive better business results, and live their leadership legacy with confidence.

Sarah McVanel, Chief Recognition Officer, Greatness Magnified

Self-awareness is perhaps the most important characteristic that truly exceptional leaders possess. Roxanne combines this concept with a heart-centered approach, elevating leaders to be more authentic and truer to themselves. In my work, I often speak to clients about the need to continuously check-in with themselves and ensure alignment between what they're saying and what they're actually doing – between values and decisions. *Return to Relationships* provides tangible examples and information on how to do just this and to evolve one's leadership in the process.

Hema Crockett, Author and Co-Founder, Gig Talent

Roxanne Derhodge has done a masterful job of describing the essential elements of authentic leadership, and presented a thoughtful and pragmatic guide for leaders.

Kamales Lardi, CEO, Lardi & Partner Consulting, Chair,
Business Forbes Council Women Executive

# ROR

## RETURN ON RELATIONSHIPS

### AMPLIFY YOUR AUTHENTIC LEADERSHIP TO CREATE MORE RESILIENT TEAMS

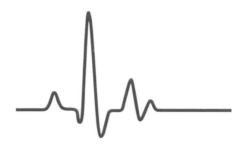

## ROXANNE DERHODGE M.Sc., R.P.

ISBN 978-0-9958678-1-9 (Paperback)
ISBN 978-0-9958678-2-6 (e-Book)

First Printing


Editor: Catherine Leek of Green Onion Publishing
Interior Design and Layout: Kim Monteforte Graphic Design Services
Cover Design: Azadeh Yaraghi of Gogo Telugo Creatives

# A Prince in the Making

A Prince in the making, a boy with a plan
Created a blueprint for his life long before he became a man.

Stood alone in a cane field at the crack of dawn
Pressed the cutlass to his chest and stifled a yawn.

Made a concerted effort to add to the family's coffers
Never compromised his values but accepted all offers.

A Prince in the making, a diamond in the rough
Never quit or backed down when things got tough.

Never looked for handouts, kickbacks or charity of any kind
His mental tenacity meant that he wouldn't be left behind.

Stood head and shoulders above his peers as
he strutted through the village
With the swagger of a peacock, he shared
tales of his rich heritage.

Blessed with the gift of the gab,
handsome and ever so charming
Quick-witted with a razor sharp mind
and a smile so disarming.

Focused on his strengths and successes,
learnt from his follies and flaws
A beguiling mix that left his competitors
gasping and grasping at straws.

Climbed the corporate ladder with a leadership style of his own
A Prince in the making, the heir to the throne.

An inspirational leader with a work ethic hard to match
Started a quality company that he built from scratch.

The personal touch guaranteed a customer's lifelong loyalty
A man of the people, he made them feel like royalty.

Turned a Mazda into a Maserati, a Lancer into a Lamborghini
Sold the dream that a Ford Escort was as good as a Ferrari!

A Prince in the making, a family man with a past
Lost loves, broken hearts, relationships that did not last.

Begged for forgiveness from those he hurt the most
Sought redemption, found salvation from
every past and present ghost.

He paid a princely sum – it's time for him to bask in his glory
A Prince in the making, the hero of this story!

Over the years Carolyn Gupte has donned many hats and juggled many respon-
sibilities in the fields of journalism, public relations, advertising and school
administration, but the most satisfying role in her professional life came about in
2018 when the title "Author" was added to her resume.

Born in Mumbai, India, Carolyn grew up in the beautiful twin-island Republic
of Trinidad and Tobago. She is a London-trained journalist whose lifelong passion
for writing led to the publication of *Love without Boundaries – the 49 year partner-
ship of Subhash and Carol Gupte* – a delightful homage to her parents – and her first
self-published literary work. She is currently working on her second book which
has been described as "a collection of rants, rhymes and random thoughts."

# CONTENTS

# CREATING SPACE

When I think of the role models I have had in my life, I realize what a true influence those authentic people were in my space. I realized that I wanted to understand all the clues that they were giving me along the way. They allowed me to grow to such a profound place that I was able to impact many others.

One such influence was Mrs. Williams, my high school Geography teacher. She embodied self-confidence. She carried herself in such a way that it was as if she glided into a room. She created a space in my class where I felt I could be the me I needed to be. At the age of thirteen, I felt this was the first exposure my genuine self had been given.

In the backdrop of my high school, she was an exception to the rule. Academics were the focal point and there was not any room for genuinely deep connection. Reflecting on the qualities that she displayed, it is clear she was able to open up a window within herself that allowed an internal reflection within me that said you are okay just the way you are, so shine your light.

As I share this story about Mrs. Williams, I realize that she showed me that it was possible for anyone to be an Authentic Leader. If these qualities do not come naturally to you, *Return on Relationships* will show you that it is possible to craft and develop these skills. Unfortunately, some of you may not have had these role models and influences along your path to develop these skills, but I am here to share that it is entirely possible for us all to lead in our authenticity daily.

When we think of "authenticity" in this day and age, we often think that it is supposed to be fluffy and soft. However, the definition is to have an internal space where you are able to connect to yourself on such a profound level that you are fully linked to the nuances of others around you. I am passionate about this topic. During a lot of circumstances in my life I could see the impact on individuals who were disconnected to themselves and the irreparable damage caused.

In the fast-paced world of the 21st century we are consistently bombarded with ongoing change. Often we will hear that the world is uncertain and change is increasing at lightning speed, but that became most apparent in March 2020, when the World Health Organization declared a global pandemic. COVID-19 has taken the concept of VUCA to an entirely different level.[1]

Generally, when we make decisions they are based on linear or cause and effect results; we consider things that are stable, predictable, simple and clear. However in the VUCA space all these variables come into play together, impacting how we function individually and collectively. Since mid-March of 2020, the world as we know it has changed and the unfolding of that change will show itself about eighteen months to two years after the end of the pandemic. We went from a relative amount of certainty, in every sense of the word, to not knowing what the next day would bring us based on the spread of the coronavirus.

After two days of being at home I went out for groceries where I was faced with the reality that I had to stand in a line for groceries – a phenomenon of this new world order. I could feel the fear radiating off the bodies of the people in line, even though they engaged in normal chatter. While collectively there was the pervasive feeling that life as we have known it had shifted and would never return, the individual needed to make sense of it all and continue with daily activities.

At an early age I could see when people were very self-focused and when others appeared to be able to connect to the people around them. I realized that I wanted to be someone who could connect to others on a deep level. I realized that the breadth and depth of relationships occurs when one is able to reach this space. I chose psychotherapy as my path to acquire the wisdom to actualize this goal.

Employees want their Leaders to be real and with realness amazing things often occur organizationally. Connection creates a space that is conducive to being more productive as each and every one of us wants to feel vital in our roles. Most Leaders demonstrate a high level of aptitude for Leadership abilities but can sometimes lack the skills attached to the softer side of leading. These skills are fundamental to the success of the Leader and the company. When Leaders gain a deep awareness of the skills needed to create an authentic space within themselves they are able to achieve amazing metrics that impact the bottom line.

As a Leader there are many pressures to ensure that the bottom line is met. If goals are not achieved, a lot of repercussions impact the entire organization. Leadership schools prepare the Leaders of tomorrow to achieve at a level that makes them viable to the market they will enter. They are well schooled in the arena of economics, human resources, accounting, finance and the like, but what is needed most is heightened emotional intelligence. An in-depth understanding of this space is must-have expertise versus good-to-have expertise.

There needs to be a definite shift where emotional intelligence becomes one of the main cornerstones of Leadership, like all the other core fundamental metrics that quantify the best skills needed for Leaders to excel. Without this shift, the old model will continue to persist which may create short-term success for some but long-term success will be elusive.

So, what are the elements of Authentic Heart Leadership that will be explored?

1. Self-Awareness
2. Balanced Processing
3. Relational Transparency
4. Connection
5. Recognition

*Figure 1*

# THE AUTHENTIC LEADERSHIP CONTINUUM

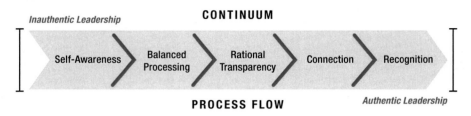

*Chapter 1*

# TRUSTING AUTHENTIC CULTURE

## The Cost of Ineffective Leadership

I had a big question in mind when I started to write about the impact of Inauthentic Leadership. What is the bottom-line cost to organizations? There are a lot of variables that go into accounting for the disconnection of employees and how these conditions impact the end result. Ineffective and/or Inauthentic Leadership is one of the biggest influences on an organization's bottom line.

There is now consistent evidence that certain work situations, including occupational uncertainty and lack of value and respect in the workplace, are associated with an increased risk of common mental disorders.[2] One of the main concerns shared by employees was the need to feel respected at work. So, if Inauthentic Leaders are not able to understand the effect of their interactions with employees, be it conscious or unconscious, this can impact the mental well-being of those around them.

Generally, most Leaders understand how they treat people directly influences them but gaining a deeper understanding regarding the level of that impact should create a bigger urgency for change. The role of

Leadership and the intent of Leadership should be focused on the importance of authentic connection and how this induces the mental well-being of the workplace.

Researchers have shown that job stress and presenteeism are positively correlated, while negative Leader behaviors have the strongest association with employee job-stress-related presenteeism.[3]

## Presenteeism

The cost of presenteeism is one of those hidden costs that is a bit hard to quantify. In the day-to-day functioning of a company it may be easier to look at the hard costs of absenteeism as there are metrics that can be tracked by various means. A business analysis would review the actual sick days, incidental absences, short- and long-term disability claims, arbitrations along with employee assistance trending reports.

However the greater cost to organizations is presenteeism, a concept where employees may fly under the radar. They are showing up to work generally but they are not being captured in some of the main reporting systems that would calculate lost productivity.

While difficult to quantify, the cost of presenteeism is estimated to be roughly 65% of lost productivity.[4] This assessment speaks to the indirect costs of disengagement in the workplace. So, how does one track this elusive lack of productivity? There are a lot of metrics of which Leadership skill is a foundational piece that, when addressed, has direct correlation to the bottom line. Leadership skill becomes very important to be able to delve into the declined productivity that may be surrounding the Leader.

So, if the Leader can skillfully understand the concerns that may be impacting their employees' levels of productivity, then they can work on that which is specifically related to connecting with their employee base. With awareness of their capacity for Authentic Leadership then Leaders are able to enhance their authentic skill set to offset the concerns that may be arising with their employees and retain their top talent.

If Leaders are disconnected from their teams, the costs can be staggering to an organization. If employees are not able to voice their concerns and feel validated and understood, these issues go underground and create a synergy of their own.

In my role as a senior executive in health and wellness I would review quarterly reports with companies. Oftentimes senior management would share that the concerns of employees were generally unfounded, however these same matters would show up as the core issues that senior management would not or could not acknowledge. The reports would reveal issues such as stress, conflict and work-life balance. The reports often highlighted the disconnection between what senior management thought was going on and the reality of the situation with employees.

The organizations that wanted to make real changes in the wellness of their employees implemented the changes needed to address the concerns but this was often not the norm. Some employers were fine with the fact that they had implemented the benefit for employees and that was the extent of what they were willing to do to address the concerns that showed themselves over and over in annual reports.

In Canada the cost of mental health in the workplace is staggering. Costs associated with mental illness (in terms of absenteeism, productivity, indemnities and healthcare) are estimated at $51 billion in Canada each year with $6.3 billion in lost productivity. The cost of poor mental health will increase to $2.5 trillion by 2041.[5] In light of this new unfolding economic age we need to be even more equipped as Leaders to address the concerns that employees bring forth.

## Turnover

What is the cost of losing a valuable employee? When considering the calculations, the bottom-line costs of hiring and onboarding can become quite overwhelming. But the costs to an organization go beyond the strict replacement numbers.

Let's say your employee earns $80,000 and you lose ten employees. That may initially appear to be a savings to the organization. It can take six months to attract and hire new talent, so strictly speaking you may think you are saving about $400,000 on your balance sheet.

"The average cost-per-hire is $4,129, while the average time it takes to fill a given position is 42 days," according to the Society for Human Resource Management.[6] Then you must factor in the impact of onboarding and getting the new employees up to optimal productivity, which some claim can take five to six months.[7]

However, there are costs in making the hire to consider that don't get recorded in the books. While the search and interview process unfold, those involved cannot be working on projects critical to your organization. Additionally, until these positions are filled, the work must continue to be performed by other employees. The stress, reduced productivity and resentment are difficult to measure.

Additionally, quantifying the hard costs of losing talent to a competitor is something that most companies find difficult to decipher. They may realize their loss as their competitors gain more market share over the following fiscal years.

So, when Leaders are able to manage more effectively they can impact some of the replacement costs and fend off their employees going to their competitors. From a business case it becomes glaringly obvious why it is vital for your Leaders to gain the skills necessary to engage, manage and retain your top talent.

*When hiring Leaders, is it about tactical skills and corporate fit or more about the skill set and needs for the future of the company?*

"Authentic Leaders, such as Mulcahy, recognize the collective power of an empowered team far exceeds that of any single individual, and they rally teams around a common cause."[8] This quote from Bill George's book describes the ability of Leaders to use their core fundamental skills to boost the power of the collective. When Anne Mulcahy became the CEO of Xerox, there was only one week of reserves before the company would go bankrupt. She inspired her team in just such a manner.

In order to engage and retain top talent, Leaders need to be the driving force that makes employees want to join and stay with an organization. If attraction and retention is not a key value for an organization, it will become increasingly difficult to stay at the top of one's industry. Gone are the days where the new generation is staying with an employer for the duration of their career. So, not only is the business case for Authentic Leadership crucial but the changing economic climate dictates that we create an environment that attracts top talent and retains them for as long as possible to stay ahead of the curve.

In order to maintain a certain level of well-being in organizations, it is important that Leaders' capacity for Leadership be assessed not just by the Leader themselves but also by their team.

## Where Are You and Your Organization At?

In order to make changes there is a need to look at where you are and this often can be a difficult space to explore objectively. We all have a bias as to how we view ourselves. It is quite difficult for us to unveil the objective truths so I think the best gauge are others around us.

Those around us are able to observe us as they are not intertwined in our internal world. Hence, it becomes imperative to measure where you are so that you do not languish in the qualities that are natural for you and also get a snapshot into your blind spots. Can this be scary? I would say absolutely. It means that we have to have an open mind about our flaws, something that is difficult for most of us to do.

In assessing the qualities of how authentic you are as a Leader from those around you, you will have to evaluate their understanding of your needs and strengths. Then as the Leader you will have to take stock of their areas of strength and where they need to foster changes to create growth in their own leadership. There is a path where your unconscious actions will emerge through the unbiased lens of your team. So, if you are thinking this will be skewed, I would agree that there may be a certain percentage of the feedback that can be eliminated or, rather, contextualized. However, definite themes will become quite apparent.

With bravery comes clarity, and I can assume that, as a Leader, you are reading this book because you want to optimize the capacity to lead and connect to others on your team.

## Elements of Authentic Heart Leadership

The core fundamentals of Authentic Leadership discuss the element of awareness but adding the element of the heart allows the Leader to take this space to a more profound level. Our bodies hold all our emotions so when we align from this space generally a calibration can occur that allows Leaders to listen and readjust their behavior on a deeper scale. With heart centered Leadership authenticity becomes further heightened.

It is the space where, when the Leader is in tune, they are able to see all the obstacles way ahead and redirect based on this aerial shot. They can make the best decisions based on all the macro and micro variables that will continually present themselves.

The skill that I think is vitally important is leading from the heart. It is imperative that those around you experience who you are as person.

Since you are reading *Return on Relationships* I assume you want to be a better Leader. Leading from the heart is not a difficult skill. It may be different from what you have been exposed to in the past but focusing on the return on relationships is more important than the old concept of return on investment. For the most part I honestly believe that most Leaders think that they lead from the heart. I do not think that anyone intentionally tries to lead from a place just within the head. I think the place of tactical outcome is a space that becomes a place of familiarity to most.

When pressures and deadlines ensue, most Leaders kick into high gear as there are deliverables that need to be attained. The trick to leading from the heart is when the Leaders are able to create a synergistic space where they are able to see clear outcomes without the failure of connection to others around them. Most people have a space that they go to when they are under pressure, but without heightened knowledge it becomes like a muscle that is familiar and reliable for productivity.

When team members feel connected they will move mountains for each other but may act defensively towards the leader if they feel a lack of connection between the leader and the team. In today's global economy there is ongoing flux that is becoming more rapid in this digital era. Leaders need to adapt on an ongoing basis to keep up and meet the diverse needs of others in their roles.

The high-level skill of leading expected from Leaders cannot be underestimated. It is vitally important to all industries where retaining one's top talent is the focal point in today's knowledge economy.

Heart centered leaders are able to effectively understand and manage the needs of those around them.

So, what are the elements of Authentic Heart Leadership that will be explored?

*Leaders who use both their head and heart are more successful at having employees buy into their company vision.*

1. Self-Awareness
2. Balanced Processing
3. Relational Transparency
4. Connection
5. Recognition

*Figure 2*
## RETURN ON RELATIONSHIPS MODEL

### Self-Awareness

The first and one of the most vitally important elements is self-awareness. This is the space that truly becomes the basis for the most dramatic growth. When you are able to deeply reflect internally into your world then you can assess your values, beliefs, assumptions and the expectations of those around you. Grasping an understanding of who you are takes great reflection. Consider the questions below; these are just some of the ideas we'll explore throughout these pages.

## AUTHENTIC REFLECTING

How do I want to be perceived in the world?

What kinds of values do I want to emulate?

How do I ensure that these values are continually demonstrated in my behavior?

What are the most important values that I need to make certain I employ as a leader?

What are the specific behaviors that I want to enhance in my Leadership?

What are the core principles that I live my life by?

Am I consistent in my actions with those principles?

Do I act the same way regardless of what is going around me?

If these questions are ones that you can clearly answer, then you may be one of the rare few who comes by this naturally or maybe you have done a lot of work as a Leader to enhance these skills. Kudos to you. If, however, you are reviewing these questions and recognize that your behavior may vacillate, this is information to note. Mastering this internal sense of awareness is a gift you give yourself. It will not only enhance your team's relationships but all relationships in your world.

## *Balanced Processing*

Along with self-awareness the next element is balanced processing.[9] This idea involves understanding someone's perspective other than one's own. When we are well rested and fully present this is often a skill that most can demonstrate, however it becomes more difficult when there are timelines, stressful elements to the day, conflicting situations among lots of other things.

How you gauge understanding someone's perspective that is diametrically opposed to your own becomes vital to growth. Often, we can become guarded if we perceive someone as always having an opposing point of view to our own. This was one of the areas that I had to work on a lot as my skill development as a mental health specialist and a Leader grew. The development was eye opening but a powerful teacher as I watched my patterns play out over and over in my interactions with various personalities over the years.

One situation that enhanced this learning was with a particular staff member in a mental health facility I ran. He was meticulous with details. If there was a microscopic detail in any situation, he could vet it out in the blink of an eye. As my learning began as a Leader and wanting to create homeostasis in my meetings, I would often divert his feedback so I could serve my agenda in meetings. This worked at cross-purposes to the overall functioning of my team. Glossing over his input and driving my agenda to move things along did a disservice to varying points of view, which impacted my vision as a Leader to serve the best and highest service of my team. A necessary lesson that I learned but it was packaged in a way that I needed to work with versus push away.

So picture yourself being able to stay present even though others may have a different point of view and still be constructive. I know that some of my learning curve in this arena was to elicit others' points of view that often varied from my own. Someone else's perspective that is different is quite valuable but gaining comfort with this stance is pivotal in your journey to heightened Leadership skills.

### Relational Transparency

The next skill that is important in the Authentic Leadership process is how open you are with relatability. Do you come across as being transparent? Are you perceived as being someone who shows how they are feeling or do you act as everything is okay even when it appears that major changes are afoot?

This is oftentimes a skill that gets misconstrued by Leaders. I need to be the rock, the one who always looks like they have their stuff together. Sometimes this quality fails you and, in fact, you need to be able to show how you might be feeling when there is a crisis. Frequently Leaders feel like they can't show their feelings as they will be perceived as weak but in fact not showing any emotions at all puts you at a disadvantage with your team. Leaders have shared with me, "If I show vulnerability I will lose my edge." Relational transparency asks you not to be stoic but be real.

If there are big changes occurring in your organization, then acknowledge it and share how it is impacting you. You might even share a story about what you have done in these kinds of situations in the past. The power of relatability is key. A skill that is not focused on in business school, it is often a talent that makes or breaks an organization experiencing massive change or ongoing competitive factors in the marketplace. Assessing this competency will help you understand where you are at on the continuum and what needs to be developed to further enhance these skills.

Is everyone sure of what you stand for as a Leader? If this question was asked of your team, would they be able to describe your decision-making process regardless of varying circumstances? In the Leaders I have worked with most would rate themselves as being good role models and felt they were able to demonstrate their values. The interesting thing is that often teams perceive their Leaders in a different light.

Leaders need to be aware of how they act when under pressure. Does your behavior change? Or are you the kind of Leader who is guided by your values and able to set aside your ego and personal agenda? From my experience, most Leaders would say they do but it is important to hear how your team rates you in this arena.

It is tough to get feedback on these skills, but at the end of the day if your score is incongruent with others around you, there is room for improvement and your team has the ability to guide your internal growth based on their feedback.

## Connection

The most pressing issue is maintaining connection in spite of deadlines and other crises. Team members need assistance with change coupled with support of their development. In my various Leadership roles I found this to be the most important skill that I needed to bring to the table when managing my team. My psychology background was instrumental and I utilized all the knowledge that I had learned to aid my teams.

I made the time to get to know each and every one of my team members. Needless to say this was not a task for the fainthearted as many times my approach was met with mistrust. However, with consistency and time it was amazing to watch what occurred when team members felt validated. As a Leader, you need a snapshot of your actual score and the reality of your scorecard from your team.

There are a lot of things that can impede this process – lack of time, ineffective legacy Leadership and loads of other pressures. Leaders who take concerted time to get to know those on their team and get a real understanding of who they are as individuals will lead authentically. This can be difficult when feeling the time pressures of deadlines, but imagine a space when investing in connection. Your growth and retention strategies are resolved regardless of the space or pace of ongoing change. Imagine a space where, as a Leader, you are able to assess rather quickly the different needs of your team during a space of massive change. The pivoting of the manager's behavior stays the course under stressful times of change and the individual needs of the team are met and outcomes are achieved. This is quite powerful to watch when a Leader is able to connect on this level.

Also, knowing what inspires your individual team members is the glue that keeps the Leader connected to each and every team member. What touches their hearts through the maelstrom of the uncertainty of change is the glue that is needed to strengthen your team. The outcome is magical to watch when this skill is demonstrated by the Leader.

## Recognition

The last element that is vitally important is recognition. All humans want to be recognized by others. In my Leadership roles, I realized that recognition was one of the most important things that each and every one needed from me as a Leader. It is frequently the small, inconsequential actions that bring the highest return on investment. Small bits of recognition are invaluable to Leaders in developing and maintaining strong connection to their teams.

Leadership, as a developing skill, is an ever-evolving process. As you grow as a Leader you become the vane that adapts to the circumstances around you. It becomes an endowment that you impart to those around you.

Gone are the days where Leaders say, "I know best and you need to follow my directions." This archaic process has not withstood the test of time. In this day and age as a Leader you have the capacity to impact each person's life. It is about having those around you feel like they are valuable and they are seen and heard in their entirety in their space at work.

No longer is there a space for Leaders who aspire to be slightly better than the most ineffective Leader that they followed. The expectation is that you leave an impression on each and every team member you come in contact with for the duration of your career. You are creating a legacy of connection and your team members will tell the story of your Leadership to others along their career path.

This is the gift of Authentic Heart Leadership. It is one that you give to yourself and those around you, which they will carry for the rest of their lives.

## TASKS FOR AUTHENTICITY

Think about what skills you look for when hiring a Leader.

Do you use both your heart and head when you lead? If not, reflect on what area you need to work on to create this balance.

*Chapter 2*

# AUTHENTICITY QUOTIENT FOR LEADERSHIP

Generally, team members may keep what they truly think of their Leaders for the lunch room or the quick interactions at the water cooler. I am proposing that we all have an Authenticity Quotient for Leadership (AQL), which is a compilation of a Leadership self-assessment and a team evaluation. This enables Leaders to get a genuine snapshot of their authenticity skills as a Leader by comparing how they perceive themselves with how their team sees them.

## Self-Perception Versus Others' Opinions

Hearing the reality of how we score on all the elements of Authentic Heart Leadership is key to making changes that are important and needed for our team. It is easy to listen to what we do well but what about the areas where we are substandard at best. It can be difficult to hear feedback about where we can improve. How do we change the core themes in our management skill set if we do not have a realistic portrait from our team?

If this conversation is making you uncomfortable, that is, I think, a good thing. We all relish in what we do well and can stay in that space without hearing the unpleasant things about where we need to grow. But if true development is to take place your team needs to be a vital part of the enhancement of your Leadership improvement plan. This may be taking you out of your comfort zone and this may create chaos on your teams, but without the openness for change there is no possibility of evolution. However, if Leadership is unwilling to show that they are capable of actual transparency, your skill as a Leader is not challenged to be the best that it can be.

*Authenticity in Leadership is the most vital thing needed to maintain productivity.*

To persuade you to undertake this challenge, let me demonstrate with a story about a less than Authentic Leader and the impact her actions had on her team.

## CASE STUDY *Inauthentic Leadership*

Maya's Leadership growth was challenged for the entire year of this consulting situation. Running a medical facility had been a career aspiration for some time, so when the opportunity presented itself, she stepped up to the challenge.

During the interview, which was quite informal, she felt an affinity to the core fundamental values of the organization. She would be reporting to the CEO and a small board. With a staff of 25, she would be responsible for an outpatient and inpatient facility.

Maya met with all staff individually and got to know each and every one of them. During these meetings, she got a sense that the CEO had his hand in everyone's day-to-day functioning. While Maya found this situation concerning, she did not see that it would be an ongoing issue.

During her first meetings, there was a definite sense of mistrust from senior staff as she started her role as Director. Initially, she felt as she was being interviewed by staff with regard to her abilities to take on the challenge of running the facility. Maya took it all in stride and did not put much stock into some of her early inklings.

She shared her concerns during meetings with the CEO, but he allayed her fears as that of growing pains with staff. Little did she know that the staff had a lot of apprehension over the CEO's Leadership style, something that would unfold slowly during weekly meetings over the next year.

Within a month, things were running quite well, but Maya soon realized that staff would take their issues directly to the CEO who obviously had a direct line to the board. She discussed her concerns with the CEO and asked that all matters related to her direct reports be redirected her way. She assumed that her conversation had addressed the issue. Unfortunately, she realized that the CEO had micromanaged the staff prior to her arrival and this was a pattern of behavior that was difficult for him to discontinue.

As the unprofessional conduct continued, Maya soon recognized that another item was contributing to this toxic environment – how her position as director was filled. The position had been promised to an existing staff member but was then filled without his knowledge. Additionally there were bigger systemic issues that had not become apparent until Maya was in the position of director. It was going to be quite difficult to gain credibility and trust when the CEO continued to undermine her functional authority with staff. It was becoming glaringly obvious that she should have listened to her gut instinct prior to taking the position.

As the year progressed there were ongoing concerns with staff and the CEO and his Inauthentic Leadership made her time at the facility unbearable. When trying to address continuing issues, the CEO appeared open but then reverted to old behaviors.

This was a situation where the level of inauthenticity bordered on being unhealthy. This company's growth was dramatically stunted due to the inauthenticity of its CEO. Needless to say, Maya tendered her resignation and resolved to listen more closely when red flags appeared prior to working with an organization.

## Organizational Readiness

When working with companies an initial assessment is performed focusing on the organization's readiness to make change for their Leaders and their teams. The company has to be equally as willing to hear the negative feedback as the positive feedback for the overall growth of the environment.

In my consulting career most companies are well intentioned but they may not be in a place where they are ready to step into a place of integrity and accountability. When this is the case, training in the arena of the Authentic Heart Leadership would be unsuccessful as what is needed most is openness and transparency. If openness and transparency are welcomed then this is the point where metamorphic change is possible to create authentic connection in Leadership.

Initially when I meet with a company, I assess, through discussions, what stage of readiness for change an organization is at. If the company is ready to make changes, then an organizational assessment can be undertaken. If they have not reached that point, then a decision may be made to work with certain parts of the organization that are struggling with their teams. It may be that an organization is not ready after a certain amount of training. In that case there may be a need to do more discovery with the senior Leadership team to clarify the goals of the organization in reference to their leadership goals.

However, if they are ready, we proceed to the organizational assessment. If any unresolved historical concerns arise during the evaluation, they will be addressed as part of the readiness of the organization for the training program. There may be times when it is recommended that the organization do some preparatory work prior to starting the leadership training program.

Once the organization is scoring in the high range for readiness and a Leader and a team want to work on making changes, the second part of the assessment begins. The team and the Leader concurrently complete the assessments based on the core elements of what is needed to be an authentic heart-based Leader. The Leader does their self-assessment and the team evaluates the Leader's skills. Both assessments are collated into a report.

The Leader is provided space to determine how self-aware they are as a leader. If, at this point, the leader starts to question what awareness has to do with the bottom line, then this may give the organization an indication of the level of skill development needed for this Leader.

The assembled report is reviewed with the Leader initially and then the Leader goes through training. The report is reviewed again as each module of skills training is finished. Additionally, the Leader's skill development would be reviewed by the team again.

The Leader is able to see the growth of their skills or the areas that they are struggling with. If the Leader is still struggling after the training modules, additional executive coaching is offered between the training sessions. Authentic Heart Leadership increases the Leader's capacity to lead their team from this new space and increases the functionality of the team as a whole.

The areas of assessment follow the elements of Authentic Heart Leadership.

- Self-Awareness – of one's self as a Leader
- Balanced Processing
- Relational Transparency
- Connection – leading from the heart
- Recognition

Each area is assessed by the Leader and the team. It is important that the Leader shares the sphere of the training program along with the ultimate goals for their Leadership development.

## Areas of Assessment

*Self-awareness* is the core, overarching foundational principle needed for Authentic Leadership.

### AUTHENTIC REFLECTING

If I am unaware of my internal space, how can I understand whether I am in alignment with the values of the organization?

If my purpose is unclear, how do I lead from a space of strength?

Most business programs are built on the tactical approach of business outcomes and often there is not much time spent on the company's values alignment and even less on the Leader's values and how this may play out in the business world. If reflection on values becomes a normative practice what may actually happen is that most Leaders would be better aligned with themselves and may make better decisions about the type of business environments that best suits who they are and their goals for their careers. This awareness, in essence, becomes a gift if done early in a Leader's career. But, it is never too late to learn about awareness as this position is needed to enhance connection and protect the bottom line.

The next core skill that needs to be assessed is the concept of *balanced processing*. That is, what is your openness to seeking others' points of view? A lot of Leaders generally approach leading from the space of an agenda where they direct the outcomes for their teams. For the most part, Leaders need to demonstrate structure for the overall running of the business, but it is important to create the room where the team is able to interject their points of view and be allowed to add to the direction established by the Leader.

If your inclination is to create a steady flow of "getting things done," it is equally important to develop a place where your team feels they can voice concerns that could be diametrically opposed to your agenda. There needs to be the freedom to obtain different perspectives in the group. If your environment is uncertain, barring some catastrophic situation, knowing what is going on in your space is key. Oftentimes Leaders are afraid that this will create derailment. Most group dissenters lose their voice as the team works toward constructive attainment of goals.

So where do you sit with this skill set? Are you able to put your agenda aside and create the space for openness? Do you get fixed on your agenda and expected outcomes for meetings? If overall you can say that you are pretty good in this arena, congratulations. But if you waver based on the tempo of the environment, then focusing on this skill development would bode you well.

## AUTHENTIC REFLECTING

Would you say that you are clearly guided by your values when you lead?

Do you have a sense of how you want to lead?

Do you ensure that all your actions are in line with your perspective as a Leader?

Are you able to share your point of view regardless of what is being shared or do you waver when there are differing perspectives from your own?

This is a goal that I think most Leaders feel they achieve but, thinking it through, do you set your agenda aside and really do what is in the best interests of your team? Having a Leadership style, where you act within your values but are still able to make it about others, requires a high level of skill. Again, under pressure are you able to connect to that deep space within yourself and make decisions based on your values? Or, do you teeter-totter? If you do, you are not alone.

Leaders sometimes try to please and make a decision based on the space within a meeting, circumventing the needs of their group. In those times, they may not be thinking of the overall situation objectively. Are you able to get to another's perspective often, sometimes or generally? Again, creating the room to come to your perspective is key. Regardless of the pressures about, when you are able to deliver on what you promise you gain a level of respect that is immeasurable. These skills will be discussed at length further along in the process.

The third quality assessed is *relational transparency*. This element is one of the most important skills that Leaders need to master. Acquiring this core element will allow people around you to develop trust, the gateway to openness and, in turn, growth within the team. Gone are the days when stoicism was rewarded as a vital quality of Leadership.

Being relationally transparent is easy when things are running smoothly but when there are ongoing changes and stressors Leaders may change their approach to manage the situation based on their level of strain. A Leader's skills may be tested in times of uncertainty as well as when there has been poor Leadership prior to inheriting the team. In the assessment, a Leader may get feedback that includes ripple effects from historical management but this can be untangled as the Leader starts to demonstrate skills of transparency and consistency.

In my early Leadership roles, I was exposed to the stoic style of Leadership and it was discouraging. I felt if this is how I needed to behave to become a Leader, then I wasn't sure I wanted to reach that level of any organization. I felt out of sync with the kind of Leader that I wanted to be and the pressures that were being imposed on me to be autocratic, tactical and disconnected relationally from my team. I was coached by the senior management team to be more authoritarian and definitely not to be vulnerable in any way, so my team experienced me as separate and apart as their Leader.

Needless to say as a young Leader it was a difficult path with a lot of growing pains. Eventually, I was fortunate to gain mentorship from some fantastic Leaders. I was able to learn that being myself was an asset rather than an impediment as a Leader.

*Leaders of the past used power to lead. Today's Leaders serve and inspire by their actions.*

*Connection* or leading from the heart is something that I often get the most push back about from Leaders. Most feel they cannot bring leading from the heart overtly to work but I truly believe that once you understand and come from that space your Leadership will be on the right track with who you are as a Leader.

In the past companies would say that employees should leave their personal lives at home. Soon, from a wellness perspective, companies realized that this was a near to impossible task. The statistics show that happier people are more productive employees.[10] So, from that slant, happy Leaders would create positive workspaces and all things would flow together for company objectives. Most Leaders and employees that I coach share that Leaders who provided a space where they were able to focus on their values and intrinsic rewards allowed them to present the best version of themselves at work.

## AUTHENTIC REFLECTING

Reflect on the various Leaders in your career.

Think back to who made the most significant impact on your development?

In March 2020, the COVID-19 pandemic hit North America and tested this Leadership skill. As unfortunate as this time was it taught me many valuable lessons, such as the strength of bonds and the need for increased mindfulness in my daily routine. As a Leader, ask yourself this question, "What have I learned about myself that impacts my perspective and style of Leadership? How am I dealing with this uncertainty?"

Creating a space of safety for your employees is paramount but the growth of Leadership during that time was being challenged on a global level. Reflecting on your mental well-being was important. What kinds of things did you implement to step up at that time? Throughout the pandemic we learned the vital importance for connection, the need to increase our capacity to communicate in dire times and the necessity to learn how to deal with fear so it does not bring us to our feet. Things such as employee assistance services (EAP) need to be front and center of organizations and it is imperative to increase connection on an ongoing basis, even when returning to the physical workplace.

Some of the amazing things that took place in order to keep employees connected were virtual coffee breaks, cooking together, virtual wellness days, yoga, taking a virtual walk together and having a family member drop in virtually, where family members get acquainted with your co-workers. Those innovations at the time showed us the need to create a more fluid space between work and home. This was a positive element that we should strive to not lose post-pandemic.

At the time of writing this book we are still in the midst of the pandemic and this time has taught us how to get more comfortable with the unknown and to pivot daily as statistics are delivered on the health of our communities.

Next we need to tune in to what *recognition* means to one's Leadership. The Leader must be able to understand the needs for recognition that exist in their teams. Unfortunately, Leaders are at such a high level of functioning generally that they may not have a good understanding of their team and what they need to be valued. We all want some type of recognition.

Oprah Winfrey shared that regardless of who she interviewed on her show, be it Barack Obama or Maya Angelou, the first question that she gets asked right after the segment is always the same.

> After every interview, you know what they would say? "Was that okay? How was that? How did I do?" In one form or another, somebody always said that [to me].[11]

Let's think about this. Some of the smartest, most famous people want feedback about how they performed, so it makes sense that we all need feedback in the form of recognition about our contributions at work. When Leaders are able to understand the core fundamentals of themselves in reference to appreciation, then they are able to start the process of gaining the data to meet the recognition needs of those who surround them as opposed to applying the best practices without consideration of what is really needed by their team and their overall organization.

In my first Leadership role I learned this the hard way. I was in my twenties and running a unit at a hospital. I was eager to do a good job. I loved my field of psychology so I wanted to demonstrate that I could apply that to all that I knew. My bright-eyed, bushy-tailed approach was quickly squashed by dissension of my team of ten clinicians. My naivety was my best teacher.

In going through the fire I learned how to become an Authentic Leader amidst the wake of an Inauthentic Leader that preceded my tenure. My values as a Leader were there but my skill enhancement started with an amazing mentor and group of clinicians. I learned to listen to different perspectives. I would often joke to family and friends that this team had a picture of me in their basements and my face was target practice with poison darts. This team and I laugh about our time together and share stories about the difficulties along with triumphs. They taught me how to live my value as a Leader and allow everyone a voice. I worked with this team for six years. It took two full years of actively applying all the authenticity skills so that upon my departure the team managed themselves and I acted as a part-time consultant.

Knowing your scorecard sets the stage for your learning.

Reviewing your assessment of your Leadership skills and then using the comparator of your team's analysis of your skills give you an honest thumbnail sketch of where you are and areas for enhancement. For details on the full assessment please go to *Roxannederhodge. com/assessment.*

 ## TASKS FOR AUTHENTICITY

Reach out to your employees in ways that show you care.

Examine and reflect on your Leadership style.

## Chapter 3

# THE HEARTBEAT MODEL

Once you gain a sense of how your skills relate to the amalgamation of your assessment along with your team's – the compilation of both assessments creates an insightful scorecard – you can begin targeting areas of growth for your Authentic Leadership.

Authentic Leadership is a body of work by Bill George. In his book, *Discover Your True North*,[12] he shares the concept that Leaders who are connected to their true authentic capacities are able to guide from a space that allows others around them to maximize their ability to function. There are many variables that impact a Leader on an ongoing basis, however when a Leader is able to genuinely be aware of their space, they are able to make the best decision regardless of dire circumstances that may surround them.

Leaders who are disconnected from their Authentic Leadership skill may have abilities to lead in the short term but in the long run their space may come into question if they do not have a heightened level of self-awareness as a Leader. Leaders who make awareness of their inner space a priority maintain a place of respect and integrity that can withstand all the stressors that most corporate environments endure regularly. An inauthentic Leader does not challenge themselves to grow consistently, which oftentimes dismantles their secure base with their teams and, in turn, the overall organization.

As I entered the field of psychology in my early twenties I started to see the importance of connection among us. I had studied all the formal literature but the real learning began when I started my first position at the Metro Toronto Police Force responding to victims of crime. This was my window into the real-life state of the human condition. The role as the trauma responder was mostly one of kindness where often there was less need for words and more need for creating a space of safety for those at their most vulnerable time.

Regardless of the positions that I have held, when those I led could sense my heart I found they showed me the most commitment. Whether running mental health facilities or consulting with companies, my role was way easier when I could create a deep connection to those in my environment regardless of the circumstances.

In my vigorous psychotherapy training, we developed skills to create a place where all client interactions offered complete connection. This space allows people to connect at such a deep level that those in these settings are able to listen to what is in their best interests at a profound intensity. Human beings are complex and when we are able to access this space within ourselves we find all the ingredients of Leadership.

The best Leaders lead from their hearts and not their heads. Tapping into one's heart creates a space where all ongoing efforts and actions reside.

## The Heart Space

The elements of Authentic Heart Leadership allow the Leader to use the heart space as the tethering spot, which heightens the level of awareness beyond the conscious mind. Self-awareness starts from the heart, then further development takes form when you go from a place of internal understanding to external application. Comprehending your intrinsic space of Leadership is the gift that guides your path to those in your circle. This relatability opens doors of deep communication and sets the stage for your knowledge and application into your model of your unique Leadership. When your heart is in tune with others, it allows the space to make clearer decisions for all involved and not just for the best interests of the few.

Starting with your Leadership story you gain a deeper fathoming of your core fundamental values that helps you conceive of who and what is important to you. How does your space inform your beliefs, values, assumptions and worldview? How does all of this impact how you lead? This is some of the most valuable information you will learn about yourself. This formulation gives you a deep understanding of why you lead the way you do. Your early story leads into your Leadership story that creates an intense awareness of your Leadership qualities and an appreciation of what you are about as a Leader.

Realizing your mission and vision provides a clarity that informs the best Leadership environments for your style along with the ones that would be most diametrically opposed to who you are as a Leader. Your corollary becomes a listing where you can reflect repeatedly and check in when you come across difficult issues in your Leadership path. Having this figured out becomes a guide post that you can refer back to regardless of the murkiness of quandaries. As your progression in Leadership occurs there comes a point where you will start to think about the legacy of your Leadership. What imprint do you want to leave behind from the lives that you have touched along the way?

As I think of my legacy, I always wanted to be thought of as the Leader who could see and grow people's potential to the maximum of their abilities. I thrived in a space where I could connect with each person's strengths and allow them to accentuate those, while recognizing their limitations and working with them to achieve the best possible versions of themselves. It has been my aspiration to make the space in the companies where I worked a bit better when I left.

*Leaders who lead with their hearts need not worry about the bottom line.*

## The Model

The step to create Authentic Heart Leadership utilizes the HEARTBEAT Model of Authentic Leadership. It allows the Leader to develop their own natural style of leading analogous to the instinctive rhythm of the human body. Your heart beat is attuned to your internal space. Leadership, when aligned with this model, achieves the Leader's optimal potential.

*Figure 3*
**THE HEARTBEAT MODEL**

## H = History of Your Leadership Journey

Understanding where you began as a Leader is extremely valuable on this journey. Oftentimes Leaders think that their Leadership began with their first job but I think that usually it starts well before this.

It is important to think of your earliest recollections. What were some of the situations that may have informed the values that you take with you as a Leader today? Stories that I often hear when coaching and speaking involve experiences that were pivotal to Leaders. What were the significant markers that need to be noted that give you a better sense of your Leadership journey?

As I reflect on my journey, one of the distinct memories was sitting with my maternal grandmother who was a guide to me and my younger sister. My parents would ask her to spend time with us and the conversations were instrumental to my growth as a little girl. When my sister and I would have spats, my grandmother would talk to us about our unique differences. My sister is just ten months younger than me. My sister was shy and I was the talker; I would oftentimes take over for her. As I reflect, this action was not intentional. There were times that this was okay but other instances where it was not. When we had conflicts, my sister's quiet demeanor did not help her.

I clearly remember my grandmother talking about how we were distinct and how important it was to respect those differences. She used the example of how we were not the same height. She looked at our limbs and shared that I would be a half-pint and my sister quite tall. At the time of these stories I did not realize that my grandmother was teaching me a valuable lesson of tuning into unique characteristics and respecting others whose makeup deviated from my own.

## E = Experiences that Map Your Path

Next looking at one's experiences in life is pivotal to your development as a Leader. Starting from your early childhood, what kinds of things would have informed who you are today? Again, there are many hidden gems that are unique to your path.

Begin with your childhood experiences. Where were you born? Was your culture an extended family setting or nuclear? Did you have an intact family upbringing or were you brought up by other primary caregivers? From a Leadership perspective most might buckle at these questions but these reflections create a space to get a real understanding of you as a Leader.

## AUTHENTIC REFLECTING

When did you have your first job and what lessons did you learn from this or other jobs in your career?

Did you formally train to take on Leadership positions or did your natural affinity create the space for you to become a Leader?

Did your skills come naturally or did you have to work hard in the positions that you held to up your Leadership game?

### A = Amplification of Leadership Strengths

What are your strengths as a Leader? There are certain qualities that come naturally to us. What are yours? Making a list of your strengths is important as it opens the window to recognize what abilities come naturally but also to the skills that do not.

Most are comfortable discussing strengths but reflection on weaknesses can be the best place to facilitate growth. Most teams are a great gauge for a Leader in this area. It is humbling to hear what you are not good at and where you need to grow to become a better Leader.

As a Leader creating a space that was conducive to open communication was something that came quite naturally to me. However, attention to microscopic detail was my Achilles' heel. This was a lesson that was imperative that I learn but it was one of the most difficult tasks to achieve. Time and time again there were countless situations where my need for detail was highlighted. Initially, my natural instinct was to distract and delay but this came with dire consequences. I butted heads again and again with this limitation but learning this skill was something that further enhanced my capacity to be an effective Leader.

## R = Reinforcement of Management Principles

There are often certain things that you learn formally as a Leader that pave the way for your Leadership. What are some of the core fundamentals in Leadership principles that have guided your path? What are some of the givens that you learned that allow you to be the best version of yourself as a Leader? Management principles usually are learned through formal education or informally through self-study. Learning from the gurus creates a steady foundation or springboard.

### AUTHENTIC REFLECTING

Outline these Leadership management principles you were taught.

How did they influence your path?

In what ways have you stayed true to these principles?

How many times have you altered them to fit your particular brand of Leadership?

When learning formal principles, the purest forms are initially needed to create a space where growth can occur.

With time I know that my utilization of certain principles has been morphed to fit my personality and styles. This becomes your unique brand of Leadership that naturally develops as you grow in your Leadership process.

## T = Transformation of Leadership Legacy

There are so many fundamental experiences that shape us as Leaders that sometimes the best teachers are the lessons from adverse situations. In considering your path as a Leader there are going to be some telling transformative pieces that allow you a bird's eye view of the actual transformation. This space will allow you to understand each and every facet, regardless of whether it was a good or adverse experience.

## AUTHENTIC REFLECTING

When thinking of your legacy as a Leader, where did you begin and where are you now?

Are there things that have stayed with you from the beginning of your Leadership journey that persist today and what has metamorphized into something different?

### B = Beliefs and Assumptions of Leadership Base

Where did you formulate your basis of beliefs and assumptions as a Leader? This can be quite the smorgasbord. Many of our experiences are a combination of our fundamental values, interactions with people and how we make sense of the world. But a lot also has to do with how our worlds, personal and professional, intertwine to create the beliefs and assumptions about how we lead others.

There is a misnomer that Leaders are different at home than at work. I beg to differ. How you run your home life is intertwined with you at work. Performing an autopsy of some of your core fundamental beliefs really brings you to an understanding of your Leadership base. It also equips you with the tools to navigate when the composition of your employee base is diametrically opposed to your values and beliefs.

### E = Experiential Development of Leadership Style

This is when you get to tune into the inner space of where your core as a Leader developed. This is where the question of who am I as a Leader emerges. This is where you get to the essential elements of what is involved with you taking care of your inner resources so that your Leadership flows from your heart.

Being stressed or out of sync with yourself directly impacts that deep place within you that contains the gifts of your Leadership. Often

Leaders may negate this space but it is vitally important to befriend it, as the more in tune you are with this seat, the better you are as a Leader. All the elements of this space pour out into your Leadership style.

## A = Attunement to Heart-Based Leadership

While spending the time in your experiential space is important, the next step is to pivot and adjust to the elements that no longer fit who you are as a Leader. This can become uncomfortable as it is new. Without these changes you become stagnant and misaligned with where your Leadership needs to go.

Leadership is fluid and needs to adapt to all the ever-changing variables that stand before you. If a Leader does not acclimate, this can cause harm to themselves and those that look for direction from them.

## T = Transformation to the Authentic Leader Within

The final task is putting all the pieces together, like mapping a journey of your own creation. This deep, arduous, revealing work will never steer you in the wrong direction. It becomes the internal GPS of your Leadership expedition that guides you so that you continually stay on track to be the best version of you as a Leader.

Often Leaders think that they have done their work when they have reached this role in their careers, but this is a myth. In order to transform into the Leader you need to be it is essential to garner information from within yourself and adjust to meet the needs of your environment. If there is uncharted territory, the captain is at the helm at all times adjusting and maneuvering to safety. The same is required of a transformative Leader. They must stay abreast of all current concerns and needs, actively participating and recalibrating, which naturally flows from that space.

It is abundantly clear that we are guided by this powerful space within ourselves that wires us to be attuned internally. This model creates the journey that allows Leaders to create the best version of their capacity as Leader. This is a path that, when explored, will bring the Leader to a deep intuitive level of their capabilities.

## TASKS FOR AUTHENTICITY

Reflect on your life story and draw out the accounts that may support some of the values that you emulate today as a Leader.

Each week, try to connect on a personal level with someone you manage. Then, notice and reflect on people's reaction toward you.

As you work through the elements of Authentic Heart Leadership, keep the HEARTBEAT Model in mind. How does each component of the model relate to each of the five elements?

# Chapter 4

# SELF-AWARENESS

Self-awareness as a Leader is the cornerstone of all change. Leaders who do not stop to reflect can create a space that will no longer sustain the growth needed in today's economic world. As you think back on your life as a Leader, it is important to reflect on what you learned along with way.

There are the pragmatics of business school, which I'm sure most of you are well educated in, but the growth part of Leadership is the hands-on approach of actually leading. The growth that occurs is often-times organic. The concerted effort to enhance your skill set as a Leader means digging into what you know about yourself.

## Your Leadership Story

*Authentic Leadership is a conscious decision to work on self-awareness.*

Thinking through your Leadership story is very important as it holds the information of the core fundamentals of your Leadership style.

I learned this lesson from my father who held an executive position while I was in my teens. He appeared to have the ability to treat everyone who worked for him with the utmost respect. Regardless of the role they played in the company, he regarded everyone as holding the same value. Seeing the way he engulfed the employees in his presence was one of the most influential experiences of Leadership

I had at an early age. He was very charismatic and was able to hold the attention of a room with his amazing oration skills, a talent that I realized was vital to Leadership in all parts of life.

My father's parents were cane farmers. They started work in the cane fields at four in the morning and my father would often help prior to going off to school. He started his working life very young due to necessity and today, in his 80s, he still has a work ethic to be admired. In recalling his values, I consider how they impacted me.

My father came from an impoverished home where, at age fifteen, he was the parent to his parents. He took on the role of financial provider for his parents and five siblings. I often try to think of what his reality was like starting out with such humbled beginnings to become a senior executive at Neal and Massy, one of the Caribbean's major automotive companies. My values were informed by understanding his path, along with witnessing his hard work and the respect he garnered not just from the hard work he performed but from the respect he bestowed on others.

Reflection on your Leadership story is important.

## AUTHENTIC REFLECTING

Where did your life story begin?

When reflecting on your father's path, how did this impact you?

When reflecting on your mother's path, how did this impact you?

What were the fundamental values that you learned about Leadership while growing up?

Did you play a sport? Or engage in any other activity where you were exposed to values that impacted your Leadership style?

Is there a Leader that you admire? What qualities do you admire the most? What skills do you emulate of this person? What skills do you want to enhance that this person encompasses?

Are there skills that elude you that you need to work on based on your upbringing?

When starting to reflect on these values it will give you a deeper appreciation of where your Leadership compass started. Understanding your journey gives you great insight into how your formative years impacted your values and in turn fuels your drive to include certain elements in your Leadership. Your beliefs, values and assumptions about life are profoundly embedded in your psyche. Exploring these elements provides perspective to your decision-making process as a Leader.

No surprise after my father's influence, one of my core fundamentals values was treating everyone with fairness and respect. At times this perspective was not well received. Working in clinical settings where the main commodity was people, one would think that respecting others would be imperative, however these settings could be more dysfunctional than corporate environments.

In various corporate environments I was directed to treated those in junior positions with less respect than I did my peers. Needless to say that attitude went against my beliefs as a young Leader. I have to admit that early in my career I succumbed to the hierarchical pressure to fit in. I always favored mentoring those who reported to me and my senior VP once said I had a gift, so I would often be assigned the brightest new MBA hires who were eager to learn. I enjoyed this role as I loved teaching and sharing in whatever way I could to those starting new Leadership roles. This value of imparting respect that I learned at such a young age, well before graduate school, was showing up again.

As I reflect on my Leadership story I can clearly see which environments fit my alignment and which ones brushed up against my core fundamental values. I learned this lesson early in my career which saved a lot of stress. This is where Gen Xs' and Zs' Leaders are further along in alignment than the generations that preceded them. They are carving out the right fit from the onset. Fit is vitally important versus career enhancement if you want to be true to yourself.

In one of my corporate positions I joined a company that emphasized all the values that were important to me. It was progressive and was the right fit for where I wanted to go in my career. This environment was a perfect situation and I was able to develop the skills and acumen to finesse the skills that enhanced my Leadership capacity. As Bill George would put it, "I had found my true north."[13] According to George, when you are able to gain a bona fide sense of internal awareness, then you are able to connect to yourself on a profound level, akin to "true north" on a compass.

My ten-year term with that firm saw multiple mergers and acquisitions with an unfortunate bitter ending. At the end I was caught up in a system that was no longer aligned with what I valued. I needed to leave, but the demands of my stage of life did not afford the time to facilitate the move as quickly as I would have liked. I needed to find my way to a new path. Foundationally this position was instrumental in my career development but no longer continued to serve the initial purpose as intended. The biggest loss was the daily interaction with my amazing colleagues.

## CASE STUDY *Leading from Service*

Interviewing CEO Shelley Butler was a joy. Not only did I gain a lot of wisdom but I sincerely enjoyed the space she brought to our interview. There is evidence that supports Authentic Leadership but spending time with Authentic Leaders really gives you a window into the magical space that these Leaders create. This was a Leader who believed in integrity and hard work.

Her Leadership story starts with her growing up, being raised by a single mom and learning firsthand the value of hard work. She never envisioned herself as a CEO but her love of the computer industry and hard work created the space for her ascension.

Shelley's Leadership style was initially quite hierarchical but she always experienced discomfort when she did not engage in a collaborative process with those around her. She learned the ropes to leading but did not find comfort until she found the right alignment for Authentic Leadership.

As she entered the Leadership environment, she learned very quickly that your job as the CEO and a Leader is to create Leaders. This was a concept that intuitively made sense to her but was not a space that she had ever experienced before. This resonated with her to such a degree that Shelley started to lead from a space of service. This space was so comfortable that it felt like home and from that point onwards she unleashed true Leadership potential.

Her teams relished the space she created and grew exponentially. The trust that was created boosted productivity to new levels. She felt uncomfortable leading from a space of power, so she aligned with her space and found servant Leadership.

*Being a true Leader is allowing others to find the Leader within themselves.*
*– Shelley Butler, CEO, Dovico*

An example of that space was demonstrated when one of her sales people explained that the customer wanted to be called by someone with a "director" designation to finalize the deal. This CEO told the team member that day, "You can use the title of VIP of sales or whatever the client needs to feel comfortable to have the conversation. You are capable of closing this deal. You are not a title. You have the ability to achieve this goal."

Shelley is an example of a CEO who led shoulder to shoulder with her team. Amazing Leadership comes from allowing others to find Leadership within themselves.

Each and every Leadership position created a foundational piece for the kind of Leader I became. Understanding your Leadership path is further heightened when you start to explore the space within your heart.

## AUTHENTIC REFLECTING

What are the foundational pieces of your Leadership growth?

What skills come naturally to you?

What stumbling blocks did you encounter along the way that impacted your growth?

"Current scientific estimates are that some 95 percent of brain activity is unconscious," says Emma Young in *New Scientist* magazine.[14]

This can include things like habits and patterns, automatic body function, creativity, emotions, personality, beliefs and values, cognitive biases and long-term memory. Hence it is important to tap into our automatic actions and make ourselves more aware of our behaviors.

## Neuroscience and Your Triggers

According to neuroscience, there are three basic parts of the brain.[15]

1. **The Neocortex:** This part of the brain is responsible for all executive functioning, so is sometimes labeled the CEO of the brain. This is the tactical part of the brain, which is where most Leaders would run the pragmatic part of their businesses.

2. **The Limbic System:** Responsible for all emotions, both positive and negative, it is also called the emotional brain. When thinking of positive memories, this part of the brain lights up, however this part of the brain also lights up when we have negative memories. So, in a split second we can be connected to an amazing memory with a loved one and the next second be teleported to a high conflict issue at work. Either way this part of the brain houses all emotions.

3. **The Primitive Brain:** Also referred to as the reptilian part of the brain, it is the old brain. It keeps all things unconscious functioning, like our heart rate and body temperature, behind the scenes without any conscious effort.

So, when we think of self-awareness it is important to recognize that all of our brains basically work the same way. If we experience a negative trigger, the Primitive Brain sends a signal to the executive functioning part of the brain (the Neocortex) that it will be shut down as it requires too much energy. Next, the triggering experience sends a message that the Neocortex is offline and there is need for the fight, flight or freeze response. Then the body adopts one of these states at which point the sympathetic nervous system (located in the Limbic System) kicks into high gear. When the sympathetic nervous system revs up the heart rate increases, temperature increases and there is increased blood flow to the parts of the body needed for defense.

Once the threat is resolved the body eventually reverts back to the parasympathetic nervous system, which restores the baseline functioning of the brain. Generally our entire system reverts back to the relaxed state prior to the incident.

During the COVID-19 pandemic, we were in such an uncertain time that the world's psyche had become saturated by total panic. Our capacity to cope was being challenged on a daily basis as events unfolded. As a human race we were being compelled to cope on a level that we had never been asked to before. When we looked around and saw that all non-essential businesses were closed, social distancing was required, family gatherings were limited to five people in total, we were unsure what stipulations would come next. Would we be forced to stay in our homes until we flattened the curve? How many waves would there be?

These fears were real but more importantly we needed to start thinking about what we could do emotionally and psychologically to combat the impact the virus was having on us in the long term. Statistics began to show that most of the deaths were due to people with immune-compromised or pre-existing conditions. Even with this information most people were in a state of fear, which we are all wired for in the short term but long-term exposure to stress is when issues will arise.

From that perspective, we needed to heed the facts and instructions unfolding with the pandemic, but we also had to start to take steps to boost our immune systems. That was something that we all had control over. We needed to manage the limbic or emotional part of the brain and exercise strategies to focus on the executive part of the brain to bolster our bodies and protect against that enemy.

Leaders in these sorts of times need to act as role models to those around you. The tidal wave continued into 2022, but what was needed most was for Leaders to show who they really were and demonstrate the principles needed to weather that one-of-a-kind storm.

## Triggers and People

Let's translate what the brain does when you are in Leadership settings where you are continually being triggered due to the ongoing demand to make decisions under stress. It becomes imperative to understand what kinds of things may trigger you, thus impairing your ability to make logical decisions throughout your day. Are you aware of what kinds of things trigger you? This is key. If not, you are leaving your day to be dictated to by unconscious circumstances.

### AUTHENTIC REFLECTING

What kinds of circumstances appear to overwhelm your capacity to make logical decisions throughout the day?

Are there personalities that you find most difficult to work with?

Reflect on your last meeting that went well. What kind of meeting was this? What elements made this an effective meeting versus ineffective?

Reflect on the last time you had conflict at work. Who was the conflict with? How was it resolved? How did you act in this meeting? Did you feel you resolved concerns in a way that felt good to you?

Based on the scenarios above, I would like you to identify the trigger, self-talk, behavior and your thoughts in each situation.

It becomes important to think of the kinds of scenarios that impact your capacity to function effectively at work. These situations have a lot of clues about the things that trigger you. It creates a basis of knowledge regarding what you might unconsciously expect of others' behavior. This insight can really create a deep understanding of your reaction when team members do not act in congruence of your expectations. Spending time with these questions will help you work it out when you have had a huge visceral reaction with a certain personality that does not make logical sense based on the context of the person's behavior.

As a Leader I had to come to terms with the fact that being detail oriented was not one of my strengths. Personalities that were microscopic would often derail my bigger-picture thinking. In meetings, these people would topple my trajectory of the overarching view and I often felt perturbed by the needs of the individual who saw things microscopically. In truth, in my early years I thought of these personalities as disruptors and not in the positive definition of the word.

As I focused on areas of enhancement needed in my development I realized that these personalities had a skill set that alluded my make up. In improving this skill set it accentuated my capacity to become a better decision-maker while boosting my capacity to be creative and innovative.

## AUTHENTIC REFLECTING

Review the case scenario of a team member as described in the sentence below and answer the questions that follow.

Envision a person on your team with whom you work very well.

What are the qualities of this individual?

How do they communicate with you? Are they logical and sequential in their thought processes? Are they big picture?

How do they add to your department? Do you know this team member well? Does this person act as a team player according to your definition of cohesion?

Do you think this individual has similar values to you? Or are they different?

Have you had to resolve conflict with this team member? If so, what was your approach and what was the team member's response?

We are often aligned with team members with personalities that have a reflective lens similar to our own. However, growth as a Leader is getting comfortable with someone whose personality and background is diametrically opposed to your own. In understanding your comfort, you need to be able to start thinking of the different personalities on your team and your relationships with them.

Now let's explore the personalities that you find the most difficult to deal with.

## AUTHENTIC REFLECTING

Think of the last couple of conflicts that you had on your team. Reflect on each one.

What were the personalities of the team members with whom you had conflict?

Are there similarities between the personalities you had conflict with?

How do you deal with conflict?

Are you able to listen to the opposing point of view of the person you are having conflict with?

Are you aware of any labeling you may do with team members who impact your capacity to treat them objectively?

Do you show favoritism to certain team members versus others?

Self-awareness will give you a snapshot of the areas that you may need to work on along with referencing your team's responses on Authentic Quotient. This will give you a true glimpse into which personality you are comfortable with and which ones you need to focus on so you maintain a constructive, neutral space when dealing with them. The capacity to treat each team member the same offers a place where ultimate trust can be developed and a high level of group cohesion can be fostered.

## Triggers and Situations

So now that you have an overview of individuals in both positive and negative scenarios, I would like to focus on a task area that will be really important to your growth. This is understanding how your triggers disarm your style of interaction. A triggering situation allows you to recognize the circumstances as such and what may be not obvious underneath it, wanting you to protect yourself.

Consciously most times it is difficult to parse out what is happening when we are being activated. Triggers can lurk in the dark and your responses can create an over-the-top reaction from you, indicating this is an area you need to explore in more depth. I will attempt to use an example to illustrate a triggering situation.

Let's say that growing up you were reprimanded and belittled for being disorganized. You had to work awfully hard to demonstrate this skill but oftentimes were not rewarded for your efforts. This negative trigger gets stored in your unconscious as something that had negative connotations in your life.

Now, let's bring this forward to the workplace and the impact it may have on your team members who are consistently disorganized. In this scenario, you may be triggered and less than tolerant with team members who are disorganized persistently. You are being set off by the lack of organization, which turns off the Neocortex shutting down executive functioning. Hence, you may be less patient or more reactive to this team member's lack of capacity to be or stay organized.

So, the process flows from a trigger (disorganization), then translates into a thought ("why don't you care"), which shifts into anger, that impacts your behavior by reprimanding the team member in front of the team. The brain has a stickiness when it feels it is on familiar ground. It protects us against any dangers as in the sequence I described. Please see below a list of cognitive distortions along with a chart for disputing them.

### *Overview of Cognitive Distortions*

Cognitive distortions are thoughts that cause individuals to perceive reality inaccurately.[16] Specifically, negative thinking patterns reinforce negative emotions and thoughts, as in the scenario around disorganization in the previous section.

Reviewing the list of distortions is important as it will give you a sense of which distortions you may have an affinity to. Most people, on average, appear to have three or four that they use the most. I would suggest that you review the entire list and then decipher which ones are your go-to biases.

1. **All-or-nothing thinking** (aka my brain and the Vatican's): You look at things in absolute, black-and-white categories.

2. **Overgeneralization** (also a personal favorite): You view a negative event as a never-ending pattern of defeat.

3. **Mental filter:** You dwell on the negatives and ignore the positives.

4. **Discounting the positives:** You insist that your accomplishments or positive qualities don't count (my college diploma was a stroke of luck, really, it was).

5. **Jumping to conclusions** (loves alcoholic families): You conclude things are bad without any definite evidence. These include mind-reading (assuming that people are reacting negatively to you) and fortune-telling (predicting that things will turn out badly).

6. **Magnification or minimization:** You blow things way out of proportion or you shrink their importance.

7. **Emotional reasoning:** You reason from how you feel. "I feel like an idiot, so I must be one."

8. **"Should" statements** (every other word for me): You criticize yourself or other people with "shoulds," "shouldn'ts," "musts," "oughts," and "have-tos."

9. **Labeling:** Instead of saying, "I made a mistake," you tell yourself, "I'm a jerk" or "I'm a loser."

10. **Blame:** You blame yourself for something you weren't entirely responsible for, or you blame other people and overlook ways that you contributed to a problem.

Once you have identified the distortions you use the most, I would recommend learning their descriptions. Learning the definitions becomes a valuable tool that you can use throughout your day. Most people have a lot of distorted thoughts that they incorporate into their daily thinking without substantiating the validity of the thought. The Buddhists refer to this as "the monkey brain."

When you are able to recognize on a more conscious level that you are distorting the perceptions of your thoughts, then the misrepresentations can be corrected to be more logical, rather than based on maladaptive patterns that often occur at an unconscious level. Discovering how to track and reinterpret how you think is the best remedy for using the logical part of the brain that assists you in staying present and aware of how your thinking can impact your feelings and, in turn, behaviors.

Once you identify your go-to cognitive distortions, you can resolve the misrepresentations. Dr. David Burns is a prominent researcher in the area of mood and his work has been formative in allowing people to work on their cognitions.[17] His remedy, New Mood Therapy, allows you to stay focused on the present and not vacillate to the past or the future. This helps you to train your thoughts to stay present and ultimately focused on what *is* rather than the interpretation we put on the thought.

## The ABCs of Cognitive Therapy

Psychologist and researcher working in cognitive behavioral therapy, Dr. Albert Ellis developed the ABC Model in 1957. Its name refers to the components of the model and assists in dealing with and adjusting our cognitive distortions.

A. **Activation:** Adversity or an activating event occurs. In this case we are looking at triggers in your workplace.

B. **Beliefs:** We put meaning to the event through our thoughts and then feelings follow the thought. This is where the cognitive distortions come into play.

C. **Consequences:** These include your behavior or emotional response. We react based on our beliefs of the initial event.

The chart in Figure 4 is helpful as you can review all your triggering events on an ongoing basis.

*Figure 4*
## TEAM MEMBER QUALITIES

| Activation/Trigger | Belief/Cognitive Distortion | Consequences/Feelings/Behaviors |
|---|---|---|
| | | |
| | | |
| | | |
| | | |
| | | |
| | | |
| | | |
| | | |

Using your recordings in Figure 4, reflect on each triggering quality from your personal perspective. When working through this exercise what perspective have you gained about the triggering qualities of your team members? Upon reflection you can then create a different narrative that allows you to have a more objective stance with the triggering event or quality of a team member. That being said, this is a difficult task when caught in the middle of a triggering sequence. Pondering scenarios that may present is a great way to continuously strengthen this internal emotional muscle of understanding.

The next step is creating a new alternative, objective way of reacting to this triggering event by being more conscious of your internal space.

## Create a New Consequence

The next step is determining what you can do to curb your reaction in a more logical and sequential way to replace your subjective interpretation of the triggering behavior. The sequence of these steps is as follows.

**Step 1.** The event occurs

**Step 2.** A thought follows to which you put meaning and purpose

**Step 3.** Based on the interpretation of the thought, feelings are elicited

**Step 4.** Based on your feelings, there is a physiological reaction in your body to the emotion

**Step 5.** Reinterpret the event based on facts versus subjective reality

**Step 6.** Outline facts to support the more objective frame of the event

*Evaluate your thoughts daily. It's the true gift of intelligence.*

Your perception of events can at times become skewed. As discussed, these are often referred to as cognitive distortions. When we misperceive scenarios it is important to straighten out these cognitions in order to create the space for a more neutral reaction, which ultimately has a huge impact on our interactions.

Creating a more appropriate reaction can be done in several ways, such as writing in a journal, using a thought log or documenting an overall reflection after an interaction that you have found difficult.

- **Journal:** You can log all the events of the day here, including all your interactions. Allow yourself the space to simply catalog all the happenings. This may be something you can use daily; you can put into a monthly log and then a year-end log. It records factual events and is often nice to reflect on as reference to achievements.

- **Thought Log:** This activity allows the brain to free flow your thoughts. Make this a daily routine. Create a quiet space where you can record your thoughts. I would suggest that you write but do not re-read your thoughts at that moment. Then, at a later point come back and re-read. This can be done daily, in the morning and/or night. The idea is to compose from a space within your unconscious so themes and patterns may repeat, allowing you to understand what may be elusive to the unconscious.

- **Reflection Log:** In this type of diary you note your subjective experiences to a situation. You reflect on your thoughts, feelings and learnings from a situation. This can also be done after an interaction that you would like to learn from or potentially what you might use when you have done some learning and reflect on what you have gained from the learnings.

According to neuroscience, mastering the techniques to alter your cognitive distortions will give you a sense of continual growth in all relationships. The process of being triggered and recognizing where it takes you, either to the past or the future, is called "dual processing." The more masterful you become in utilizing these steps, the less time you will lose when triggered. Being able to pivot back in less time is the ultimate goal with this process.

Throughout my years of coaching, clients have uttered this desire, "I wish I could learn how not to be triggered again." As nice as it is to think that you will never be triggered again, your brains and bodies will protect you till you die. However, your reactionary capacity will come in line with your inner state. The more you work on your capacity to control your thoughts, the better you will be able to play the observer and impact the best possible interactions in most circumstances.

Your ability to channel your behaviors to the highest magnitudes enables others around you to expect a certain level of decorum from your behavior. Once your teams are able to see that you use a high level of skill to understand their needs then the rudimentary elements of trust start percolating. Initially, as a Leader you will be tested as this is a normal and natural part of the process as your teams get to know you. It is important that you demonstrate the ability to show that you are willing to learn about everyone on your team and learn what is needed to establish a firm foundation as a team.

In teams the importance of trust cannot be underestimated. It is vitally important for your entire group to feel like they are being treated with the same demeanor across the board. If there are historical concerns on your team it is important to vet them early and address them as soon as possible. If tensions are unresolved they can go underground and derail the entire process, which creates an unhealthy energy of its own. Your Leadership is key to demonstrate your ability to decipher when things are awry and create the space to make real and beneficial changes.

## Being Alert to Stress

The cost of stress to American businesses is estimated to be 300 billion dollars, according to the World Health Organization.[18] In my sixteen-year role as a Health and wellness executive, I managed over seventy-five companies. I saw firsthand the reasons that caused employees to have concerns, impacting their capacity to work. I found that the definition of stress was as varied as each person's perception of events, and as Leaders you need to be aware of your stress as well as that of your employees.

Regardless of the size of the company, sector, geographic location or demographics, there were pervasive themes trending year over year in analysis reports. I analyzed the reports quarterly, semi-annually and yearly for the companies so they could understand the key cost drivers that impacted their employees' ability to stay at work. The most pervasive themes were related to relationships, personal stress, workplace stress, mental health, parenting and work-life balance.

Upon reviewing the reports, recommendations were made to the company about the strategies that needed to be implemented to keep their employees at work. The trending analysis of access to employee assistance services (EAP) would range from 5-15% where sectors like healthcare would be on the higher end of utilization. Year over year, although trending would be consistent, short-term and long-term disability would continue to rise when companies did not address concerns being identified by the trending analysis of their employee base.

There was a certain percentage of the population, regardless of their ongoing concerns, who would never miss work but functioned at approximately 65-75% of their capacity, which is commonly referred to as presenteeism. The greatest cost to employers is around short-term and long-term disability claims coupled with the financial implications associated with lost productivity due to presenteeism. Leadership can become quite instrumental in reducing these huge overhead costs. A Leader's awareness of the implications of stress starts with the Leader's own mindfulness and this sets the stage on how to effectively manage stress to optimize functioning most effectively.

### Types of Stress

There are two kinds of stress – eustress and distress. Eustress, or good stress, is noted less frequently and is credited for motivating you to achieve your goals. Eustress is the ticker that allows us to give meaning and purpose to things that we find important in our lives. We all need a healthy dose of eustress and most senior Leaders can access this positive part of stress due to their tendency to be purpose driven.

However, most of us are more familiar with distress, the negative end of stress. If unaddressed, it results in emotional, psychological and physiological impacts.

We are wired to cope with short-term stressors but the concerns that bear upon us most are long-term stressors that are not effectively addressed. Over the years in my clinical practice, I found that senior Leaders who sought services for short-term stressors but did not make the necessary changes needed would often return years later. By this time the issue had developed into a chronic problem. This is a fairly normal pattern seen at the senior level of management in private practice.

It is important for Leaders to address these organizational concerns so they can circumvent the millions of dollars lost due to incidental absences and the unresolved short-term disability claims. That being said, you will not eliminate all stressors but you can create a healthy approach to effectively manage it. Your competence to manage your stress trickles down from you to your senior management teams, then to their teams and followed by the front-line employees and ultimately to customers and external suppliers.

### *Managing Your Stress*

So, what does it takes to manage stress effectively? The medical model of stress once thought of the brain and the body as separate entities – an archaic notion. Neuroscience and psychology have proven that the brain and the body are one in the same and have a symbiotic relationship. The most effective strategy of care should always involve both the brain and body in concert.

When an event occurs, the brain interprets it as safe or unsafe at which point the brain then signals the body to enter either relaxation or protection mode. This is the flight-or-flight response that our system fluctuates through constantly. Where there is a perceived threat the executive functioning of the brain shuts down and triggers the sympathetic nervous system, pumping out stress hormones to defend the body against the attack. So, think for a second how often you might be in that fight or flight state and what impact might it be having on your body and brain.

Gaining an appreciation of your stress level becomes a guidepost to understanding what is needed to effectively manage things on an ongoing basis. Mindfulness is key to being able to handle this cycle so it does not become detrimental to your overall health. This skill strengthens in power just as our physical muscles gain strength and resilience with an increase in reps. It has a domino effect too. The earlier you catch the behavior, your ability to slow down the intensity of your reaction becomes easier with repetition.

Here is an example of a Leader who did not effectively control her stressors whenever there was conflict with her staff. When a contentious issue arose in meeting, this Leader would become flooded, visibly defensive and she would show indecision in her meetings. Her doubt undermined her credibility and created a place of uncertainty where certainty was needed. The dissenters utilized this space to corrode the already low confidence on her teams. What was needed was self-reflection to understand the patterns of the triggers around conflict and use strategies to abate those triggers when there were different perspectives in her meetings.

So, what does mindfulness have to do with management anyway? It is the skill that allows you to tame the inner space of your thoughts and lead from the place of the watcher of your thoughts. It is the capacity to use all five senses continually and to accept that triggers will be managed but never eliminated totally.

It is meant to assist Leaders in harnessing the space between triggering scenarios and creating a gap to deliver the most authentic reaction possible, regardless of the situations that present themselves in your life. Let's review what it means to be mindful and start to discuss your mindfulness story.

## Mindfulness

Mindfulness is the gift you give your inner Leader and true authentic self to understand your shortcomings as a Leader. Many may think that mindfulness means going on a retreat to the Himalayas. This is far from the truth. It is a skill where you use the capacity of your senses to temper the mental street brawl in your head. So, let's get into what mindfulness is and what it is not.

## *What Is Your Mindfulness Story?*

It is important to look at *your* understanding of mindfulness. On Google there are millions of definitions of mindfulness. What becomes important is to take a picture of your mindfulness story. This means reviewing what sorts of things might you engage in daily to manage yourself. It can be difficult to know what you may need to do for mindfulness but it becomes easier when you determine what stresses you on a difficult day. So, let's work through your most recent stressful day and deconstruct the stressors.

To review all the elements of that day, answer the questions below in as much detail as possible.

- Did you sleep the night before? If so, how much sleep did you get? Was it restful sleep?
- Did you have anything to eat or drink prior to bed that may have impacted your capacity to have a good night's sleep?
- Did you dream?
- When you awoke, what was the first thought in your mind?
- Next, think of the actual routine of your day. What was your morning routine like?
- Did you have breakfast?
- If so, what did you have?
- What was your itinerary like for the day?
- Did you have a fully scheduled day?
- Was the flow of your day pretty typical or were there lots of unforeseen disruptions to your normal schedule or routine for the day?
- Were there any conflicts during the day?
- Did you have lunch? If so, what did you have?
- Did you take any breaks at all through the day? If you did, how many and for how long?
- Did you have any last-minute changes to your schedule?
- How long was your day?

- Did you exercise that day? If so, what type of exercise did you do? And for how long?
- How long was your work day?
- What was the routine like when you got home? Did you spend time with your family?
- What was your evening routine like? What did you do to relax?

These questions give us a measurement of what a difficult day is like for you. In gaining an understanding of your stressors, it becomes easier to address these concerns and tailor your mindfulness to circumvent your ongoing agitations and manage your schedule effectively. The idea is to have an internal benchmark so that you can replenish throughout your day, instead of waiting for the perfect opportunity to have an hour to practice mindfulness.

According to neuroscience it is about staying present when the sympathetic nervous system catapults you out of the present due to the body's protective tendencies to keep you from imminent danger. As a result of your biological functioning, you are constantly scanning for things that could go wrong because of your anthropological underpinnings to keep yourself alive – the residual effects of your ancestors warding off saber-toothed tigers in the wild. Your brain cannot delineate the difference between life-threatening triggers and a difficult employee. Your skills have to be at a commensurate level so when the physiological shift occurs, you can help the brain use the most appropriate strategy to match what you are dealing with.

### Internal Awareness

On a routine basis it is necessary to scan your five senses as an indicator of how present you are.

As a young mother and a corporate executive, at times my days were fourteen hours in length. My night was constantly disrupted with feedings coupled with a day full of meetings, as well as a three-hour commute. Those were some of the most difficult times of my career. I cherished being a mother but I also loved being a corporate executive but my stress levels were through the roof. At one point my face and eyes blew up like a balloon. My stress was so high that my body started to defend against it.

Initially, the doctors thought it was allergies but soon concluded it was my lifestyle stressors. I was given an EpiPen in case swelling started in my throat. This was an eye-opening experience. My body was guiding me to create the homeostatic balance I needed to regain my health. This realization created the space to make the change to work virtually, creating more balance. Once all the adjustments were made there was never the need to use my EpiPen.

So, what constitutes mindfulness or internal awareness? Visually our eyes are the main sense we use to maneuver the world. Frequently, we are on automatic pilot and do not reflect on what is around us on a routine basis. Occasionally we gently pause on our walks to reflect, perhaps on the weekends. Most times we gloss over things that are around us regularly.

But what if you were simply to stop right now for a moment?

## AUTHENTIC REFLECTING

I want you to look around the room that you are in and name objects that are in that room.

Take the time right now and name some of the objects; look at the object like it is the first time you are seeing it.

Describe its texture. What does it feel like?

Is it heavy? Light?

What color is it?

What is its shape?

This exercise encourages us to see how many items are around us but that we gloss over on a routine basis. Mindful watching increases your ability to be the watcher of your world from a different lens.

Mindfulness watching became the basis of my internal awareness when my son was a baby. In taking in each and every moment in his presence I was able to stay completely present and look at my world with all my senses. So, your task is to find times throughout your day to practice being mindful using all five senses. This will allow you the pause needed to recalibrate your internal space to one of stillness and where you can look at your interaction with the world.

We have internal awareness, which is thinking, intuition, feelings, and body sensation, coupled with physiological awareness, which is seeing, hearing, smelling, tasting and touching.

*Slow your mind as often as possible so you can tap into the inner wisdom of your internal world.*

The internal world is where you learn things about yourself, like who you are. This is the place where you get to the deep, reflective questions of life. This is the space where you come to terms with your values, beliefs and assumptions, which start from conception and continue throughout your life. When you can align to that deep intuitive space with your external reality, then your actions become more congruent with your meaning and purpose in every arena of your life.

There is a myriad of methods to achieve this state, but we will explore a few techniques for you to consider trying.

- **Belly Breathing**: This is a basic exercise that can be done anywhere. This style of breathing will bring you back to natural homeostasis. The idea is that when you inhale fully there is full rising of your lower abdomen. Generally when stressed inhalation is constricted, the air is compressed in the upper chest. A trick that helps is to put one hand on the upper chest and your other had on the lower abdomen. When you inhale you will feel the lower abdomen rise and then fall back on the exhale. With the belly breathing you are oxygenating your brain, which makes your capacity to think clearer; when under stress the lessened supply of oxygen creates grey, distorted thinking. Set an alarm on your phone for the morning, mid-morning, mid-afternoon and before bed to do this exercise. When done correctly you will feel a bit light-headed. So, if you are experiencing this, you are on the right track. Make this a part of your daily routine.

- **Visualization:** In the beginning this should be done with guidance. There are numerous apps that can guide you using images like the beach, mountains and various terrain. This exercise starts off with regulating your breath, followed by a visual journey into a favorite landscape. My beloved place is Mayaro, a beach in Trinidad and Tobago where I spent summer holidays with my family and friends. Initially I would suggest you use an app or record your own voice describing your favorite place. As part of this exercise, you can ground your image with an object that you wear all the time, like a ring or chain. As you guide yourself through the visualization, you can touch the object that you want to anchor you to your image. With time you can touch that object and your mind and body will recall all the sensory information to take you to that chosen place. This exercise can be used when in stressful meetings and no one would be the wiser.

- **Progressive Relaxation:** This technique combines a breathing exercise as you are guided to tense various muscles from the top of your head to your toes. At the start you are directed by your breath and then progressively you are guided to tense every part of the body for a couple of seconds and then you release. As you progress, you become aware of which parts of the body hold the most tension. Because you are exaggerating the tension eventually you are completely relaxed at the end of the exercise.

- **Sensory Suitcase:** The last technique that I developed is an exercise using all your senses.

- Initially, I ask what images come to mind when you focus on what is important in your life. Generally, people pick children, grandchildren, parents, beaches, pets, etc. Pick the thing that comes to mind and find five pictures. Make a file of these pictures on the home screen of your phone. Next, what music makes you want to dance or just makes you happy? I would like you to make another file on your phone of four to five songs. Next, what texture do you like? Cotton? Satin? Find the texture you love and cut a small swatch that you will keep with you. Now, what scent makes you feel completely relaxed? Find this aroma in candle form. When you light it, you can take in the bouquet and become reoriented to the present moment. Finally, what taste makes you feel happy? I suggest that you find a gum in that flavor. If not, buy a really intensely flavored gum and use it for this exercise.

- Set an alarm on your phone to sound several times a day. At those times, you will follow the sequence of steps for this exercise.

- Starting with the visual, you are going to slowly go through the images on the file you created, one at a time. You are going to reflect on the picture – the what, who and where of the picture? How do you feel in the picture? Do this for all of the pictures. Next, listen to each song on the playlist you downloaded. Reflect on each song and take in all the nuances. Next, I would like you to take the scent that you picked and apply it to the swatch of material you chose. Then, you are going to smell the swatch and feel its texture several times. Finally, you are going to take a piece of the gum of your choice and chew it, taking in all the sensations that come into your mouth with each and every bite.

Doing this exercise will bring you back to the present regardless of the stressors that you may experience throughout your day.

Choose a couple of exercises that resonate with you and practice them as often as you can throughout your day. Depletion is circumvented when these exercises are done regularly. Understanding your internal space is one of the core fundamentals that is needed so you always have a baseline for where you are. This state dictates your internal compass so you can effectively deal with the external world.

## *TASKS FOR AUTHENTICITY*

Take a moment today and be aware of someone who is different from you. Try to gain a better understanding of their differences.

Monitor and journal your events, thoughts and behaviors daily.

Challenge yourself to quieting your mind on a daily basis.

As you reflect back on the concept of awareness as a Leader, how did you rate yourself and how do you believe others on your team would rate you? This is the beginning point of exploration and, in turn, growth.

## Chapter 5

# BALANCED PROCESSING

Balanced Processing is the space a Leader comes from based on a lot of variables. It is awfully important that Leaders ensure that this vane is clear and work to accommodate this place continually. If the Leader is easily deterred or distracted and reactive based on what is going on externally, then decisions can become dictated by this reactivity.

I am not suggesting a noticeable space but one where, lurking in the recesses of your mind, your moral compass may be impacted. So, doing this kind of internal work affords the room to continually purge, reconnect and then re-access based on the cumulative stressors that can occur in your life at home or at work.

### AUTHENTIC REFLECTING

Is it natural for you to create self-assurance within yourself?

Is it a hit or miss scenario?

What is your reliability index when it comes to yourself?

When thinking of integrity as a Leader, there are some fundamental considerations. Once you have figured out what you need to fill yourself emotionally, next comes decision-making from the moral position. One of the most vital elements in this process is self-trust.

## Integrity

Authentic Heart Leaders need to harness and build up these main traits in order to create that circumstance for trusting themselves.

- Follow through
- Credibility
- Fairness
- Consistency

When Leaders are unable to trust themselves on follow through, this becomes the frame within which they gauge others. The ability to afford others that space means starting with yourself. As a Leader your actions are under constant scrutiny. The best-intentioned Leaders can fall prey to how their incongruent actions may start to impact their perceived integrity.

### Follow Through

How well would others see you demonstrating your follow through? Are your actions in line with your words?

In one of my consultive roles, I was asked to go into the hospital to offer support to employees during the SARS Epidemic in 2003. My son was immune compromised with pneumonia at an early age, so I had massive concerns about my presence at the hospital. These concerns were conveyed to my senior Leadership team and another consultant was sent on behalf of the company. The need for additional support grew at the hospital and my assistant was informed that she would also need to attend on behalf of the company.

My heart sank as my assistant also had a young son, just a couple of months older than mine. Immediately I voiced my concern requesting that my assistant be given the same consideration afforded to me.

My decision to support my assistant rippled throughout our team and the organization, creating a space of safety. Senior Leadership gained a level of trust that allowed all the consultants to perceive the senior team as having their best interests at heart.

When reflecting inward do you follow through on things that are important to you, for you solely? It can be as simple a declaration as "I am going to exercise daily," but when the time arrives there is always another option. The promises made to yourself are equally or even more important than promises to others. Follow through builds the internal emotional muscle that says, "I am important and valuable." Keeping promises to yourself creates a space that also allows the same space for others.

Most Leaders are generally very high achievers in reference to work but self-care may be less important on their priority list. What expectations would you have of your teams and their behaviors if they were in the same predicament at work? Do you trust that others would follow through or do you micromanage to ensure things less significant get done? I am not suggesting accepting substandard levels of performance but it is important to have a certain level of trust that employees can prioritize their own work flow.

Perception in your ability in this area might be difficult to measure, so approaching others who know you well may be the best place to start garnering information. Getting feedback from family members on their perception of you in this area can be very illuminating. The Authentic Quotient provides an assessment of how you might place in this area, however closest friends and family may provide the most realistic ranking in the area of integrity.

Consistency is key in getting buy-in from others around you. So, follow through with yourself is the first source of information and consistent follow through with others is the second rung of the ladder. If you are pretty good with following through with yourself, then can others expect that you would do the same for them?

## *Fairness*

Another important element of integrity is displaying the behaviors that demonstrate your willingness to roll up your sleeves and jump into the trenches to assist others. Some Leaders demonstrate a lack of credibility by having different standards for themselves as compared to others.

As a manager at a hospital in my early career, our management team held our monthly meetings at Arabella's Tea House, a quaint little place where we could have the privacy to discuss business in a beautiful backdrop away from the weary walls of the hospital. Other groups in the clinic were very distrustful of these meetings and there would be rumblings upon the return of senior management from these biweekly meetings. There were comments like, "Isn't it nice that they get to sneak off and have tea and crumpets whenever they like on a Friday afternoon." There was a sense that the senior team could go have fun and other staff were not afforded the same privilege.

*Authentic Leaders continually gauge internal and external space when making all decisions.*

Being the newest member of the team, I could sense the dissension in the environment. Senior management had been remiss in addressing some historical concerns that clearly had permeated the staff's level of trust in their Leaders. The perception of these gatherings was clearly giving all the signs that this senior team needed to demonstrate transparency as an act of reestablishing trust.

Congruence in behavior becomes vital to the strength and health of an environment. The military demonstrates this attitude impeccably well where the Leader ensures safety of the entire unit before themselves.

## AUTHENTIC REFLECTING

How congruent are you with those on your team?

Are you willing to get your hands dirty with your team and demonstrate that you are all in it together?

### Credibility

The issue of credibility can be demonstrated in many ways. One of the obvious is following through on the role you were hired for. Some Leaders may be likeable but are unable to show up with the skills necessary when team members may need them most. A colleague shared with me a consulting situation where the CEO clearly lacked credibility.

## CASE STUDY *Credentials but No Credibility*

He had all the credentials and skills necessary to have been taken on in the IT sector. His CV was quite extensive. He seemed the perfect fit as the interim CEO to deal with a merger/acquisition that had been poorly managed.

The staff were very guarded due to various factors, including past toxic management practices and having a new CEO. The CEO was aware of the pre-existing concerns but had a firm plan of approach.

The new Leader came in and rolled out a plan that involved a massive reorganization where all staff would have to reapply for their current positions. When the plan was delivered, the CEO made a decision that, in retrospect, could have built core trust. However, keeping in mind that trust was almost non-existent, what he did next impacted his overall credibility as a Leader.

Based on his meetings with the frontline staff he decided to completely change his plan of action and go back on his original decision. He kept everyone in their original positions. This feat had a domino effect throughout the organization and made the staff perceive the CEO as lacking in strength. His action was based on kindness but destroyed his credibility as a Leader.

Because of the Leadership that preceded him, what was needed more than ever was a sense of safety and consistency in his conduct. Here the Leader did not trust his internal space and because he had to perform in a public arena of mistrust, irreparable damage was done. The pressure felt by this CEO altered his decision-making process which then crippled the staff's ability to respect him as a Leader.

Knowing yourself internally allows for the best decision-making regardless of the pressures in the existing setting. His initial plan may not have made him the most popular but it would have garnered much needed trust in that organization. Connecting to your core fundamentals as a Leader involves making tough choices and then sticking to the plan of action as laid out.

### Consistency

Consistency in actions builds credibility and this in turn builds the basis for trust. The less often that staff have to second guess what route you may take in making decisions, the better the space for the entire environment.

Ghandi was the master of living in line with his core fundamental principles. Frequently asked to speak on the spur of the moment, he would complete an impromptu talk for upwards of an hour. As a keynote speaker I am in awe when I hear this. It is said that he was so aligned with his beliefs that he could orate for extended periods of time and not deviate off course. His beliefs and values were so pronounced that he spoke from a deep internal space that housed his life mission.

Authentic Leaders like Ghandi are a symbol of what is possible when you master your core internal space. Leadership alignment and story is a place where you can ensure that you consistently demonstrate who you are a Leader.

## Corollary of Your Leadership

Another way to bolster your Leadership alignment is spending time to create your vision and mission statements. Whether it is in the corporate sector, home or community, how do you show up? Let's start with exploring the vision statement.

### Vision Statement

A vision statement is generally emotionally charged. It entails having an inspiring tone. It not only speaks to your present state but also to future ones. A vision statement does not include actual actionable steps but is in line with a statement that you could use as a morning declaration. It could be described as your rallying cry when things are a bit dismal or challenging.

## AUTHENTIC REFLECTING

What is your favorite part of what you do as a Leader?

Is this favorite part a driving force behind how you act as a Leader?

If not, what are the driving forces behind who you are as a Leader?

Of these, what are the most important ones?

If you look at the need that you as a Leader fulfill, what would be your goal related to filling that need?

These questions will help you whittle down to the core fundamentals of why you do what you do. This statement will be something that you can revisit often to stay the course.

My vision statement involves having everyone that I come in contact with develop their authentic voice in their roles. At times in my various positions I would have to revisit my vision statement, especially when I was going through mergers and acquisitions. When the environments were at their most chaotic and stressful, I would reflect on my statement so I could be the best version of myself in my present role that I was currently fulfilling.

Next let's review your mission statement as a Leader.

### Mission Statement

A mission statement concerns who you are doing this for. It speaks to standards and should feel unique to you. A mission statement represents the realistic mode upon which you operate.

Thinking through these questions (below) you will have all the necessary steps that you need to take to achieve your goal as a Leader. Contemplating these tasks would make sense as you prepare for your various weekly and monthly meetings. As organizational changes occur and there are shifts in the marketplace, aligning with these changes assists you in reconnecting with the steps needed to keep true to your mission statement.

## AUTHENTIC REFLECTING

What is the simplest way to describe what your Leadership style will achieve in the organization that you work for?

As a Leader, who do you serve? What are the core fundamental needs of the employee base that you are currently attending to?

As a Leader what is the core issue(s) that you resolve in your role?

In the current environment that you operate, what is the core problem that needs to be addressed?

How does the core issue in the organization impact your capacity to lead effectively?

My mission statement is acting in a way that is congruent with using my voice to align with who I am as a Leader and ensuring that I am doing the same for others. Surveying my path ensures that I am on course at all times and if there are detours along the way that I redirect the route. I am a Leader who continues to strive to demonstrate authenticity to myself and all that I serve.

Who you are as a Leader will show itself naturally as you do the work within yourself. You know who you are as a Leader by first working on that space in yourself to show that you are congruent with who you say you are as a Leader and through all the things that you demonstrate in your day-to-day actions. This will create the place for your Leadership to grow. Your decisions, actions and behavior will continually show you as the Leader you are in your own authentic skin.

So, with reference to balanced processing, what are the core fundamentals that drive your Leadership style? Thinking this through may be helpful as you start to write your Leadership story. In essence, an Authentic Leader is so connected to their moral compass that they live out what they believe as a natural extension of themselves. It becomes difficult for an Authentic Leader to lead if an environment is out of alignment with their core rudimentary values. Being in a dysfunctional system would not be something an Authentic Leader could tolerate for any extended period of time. Moral maturity is a basic tenet to Authentic Leadership. How can one be self-aware, relationally transparent and use balance processing without a positive personal value system? This would be an impossibility for the truly Authentic Leader.

## TASKS FOR AUTHENTICITY

How often do you check in with yourself to ensure your decision-making is supported by your internal moral compass?

What rituals do you use to ensure that your actions are in line with your ongoing decision-making in business?

What steps do you take to rectify a decision if you recognize it is out of alignment with your Leadership space?

What clues within your internal space indicate the need for you to spend time in quiet to attune to the decision you are about to make?

Are there specific rituals you partake in to make certain all your decisions are aligned with your core fundamental Leadership values?

What are the best decisions you have made as a Leader? And what did you learn about yourself in that process?

What were the worst decisions you have made in your Leadership roles? How did that impact you from that point onwards?

*Chapter 6*

# RELATIONAL TRANSPARENCY

When Leaders are able to connect on a deeply profound level to who they are as Leaders, then they are able to continually work from that deep space to coordinate the interactions that may vacillate around them. When working through the HEARTBEAT Model, Leaders are able to understand themselves and allow the room for others to feel safe and comfortable and open up to them. If this interactional place is devoid of the Leader's fundamental need to foster the openness of sharing, then transparency between the parties can be blocked and this may work at cross-purposes to growth.

## Communication

Most Leaders have a certain level of skill in the area of communication but what sometimes comes into question is their level of skill when dealing with contentious concerns or tapping into their internal awareness.

Communication is a skill that we learn as soon as we are born. As babies we are born into the world using our various cries to educate those around us about our needs and desires. My years of experience as a psychotherapist have shown me over and over again that our life circumstances impact our capacity to communicate.

When you think of your communication style, are you able to articulate your message regardless of the circumstances that surround you? If you can answer with a resounding "Yes!" my hat goes off to you. Unfortunately, a lot of people tell me that their styles fluctuate, depending of the scenarios that present in their day.

So, let's get a benchmark for the two types of communication – verbal and non-verbal.

### *Verbal*

The most significant part of verbal communication for an Authentic Heart Leader is listening. Let's drill down into some of the different nuances of verbal communication.

### AUTHENTIC REFLECTING

Are you able to focus all your attention exclusively with the person you are in conversation with?

Are you able to make eye contact without feeling uncomfortable? If you are distracted what strategies do you use to pivot back to the present?

Are you able to ask the right kind of questions if you don't understand what the person is saying?

Are you able to ask clarifying questions to get back on track?

Are you the type that is able to curb your enthusiasm in a conversation and wait till it is your turn to share?

Do you find that as a thought pops into your head you need to share it immediately or are you able to wait for the person to finish speaking to share what came to you?

Are you able to repeat what the person said in your own words to demonstrate that you get what they are saying?

Regardless of the kind of speaker, we can sometimes get lost in the conversation. When we are unable to show interest in who is speaking, it will distract the speaker. You may not be listening fully because you are preoccupied with your response to the content that the person is sharing.

So, how do you listen completely to capture the total message being shared while tracking your space internally so you are ready to respond when it is your turn to converse? It is important to be present to capture an all-encompassing sense of the person speaking.

Gauging oneself in this arena is important as most Leaders believe they are better communicators than they really are, according to reports from their employees. These skills are simple but at times they are not easy. In reviewing the basic definitions needed for effective communication as a Leader you can start to understand what areas you are competent in and what areas need enhancement.

Here are some basic definitions for review.

- **Paraphrasing:** This is when you use your own words to summarize what someone else has said. You should not repeat their exact words but get as close to the original message as possible.

- **Clarifying:** This is when you take the content of a message and reformulate it in your own words to ensure you understood the sender's idea.

- **Reflection:** This is when you highlight and mirror the communication to reflect what somebody is thinking, inferring, understanding or trying to express.

These are skills that can be rehearsed frequently and we can always stand to improve on them. The more you practice, the more skilled you will become regardless of the situation you are in.

## Non-Verbal

I think most people would say they communicate better verbally than non-verbally. As important as verbal communication is, the higher skill set sits with non-verbal communication.

There is a lot coming at us when we communicate. There are all the words being said, the meaning of the actual message, the person's delivery and non-verbal cues that are often laden with content. There is so much to take in when engrossed in a conversation; it takes a lot of skill to be able to decipher all that is being transmitted.

As a psychotherapist I have developed a high level of proficiency, where at times it can feel as if I am not listening to someone's spoken words but listening to their body language. In fact, it was a skill that I would often practice as an intern to see if I was able to decipher someone's body language without hearing their words.

Humans are usually unaware to what extent their bodies give away their message when communicating. What is important is to get to a point where you can ask the right questions when you feel out of sync in a conversation. If you are mistuned in a conversation there are often a lot of things that go unnoticed that can be vitally important to move the conversation along.

The elements of non-verbal communication that are important to track in a conversation are detailed below.

- **Eye Contact:** When having a conversation, how comfortable are you with eye contact? This is a skill that is crucial to becoming an effective communicator. Getting a sense of your comfort level becomes something that will really help you grow. The enhancement of this skill will create a significant return on all your conversations. Your comfort or discomfort drives the authenticity of the exchange.

- **Pace or Speed of Speech:** What is your pace of speech like? Do you find that you are able to maintain a steady pace or are there fluctuations in speed based on the interaction you are having? In understanding your pace, you are able to know yourself better and able to adjust accordingly when needed in stressful and/or uncomfortable situations.

- **Crossed Arms or Legs:** Are you aware of your body and the body movements of others you are in conversation with? If someone across from you appears to be shielding their body by being closed off, do you notice this and inflect this into the conversation? Do you bring the body language into the conversation in a non-descript way or do you ignore it?

- **Posture or Body Position:** Being aware of posture and body positioning tells you a lot about the person you are interacting with, and likewise for you. Are you holding your body a different way when dealing with a high conflict situation or when a contentious team member approaches you? This is vital information to be aware of.

- **Facial Expressions:** The expression on your face has a thousand words attached to it. How is your face projecting what is on your mind? How are you reading what is on someone else's face? If ignored this can be detrimental to the interaction and tempo of the conversation.

*Non-verbal communication cues are the secret to mastering effective, authentic communication.*

As you think of your communication skills what was the path that made you become the communicator that you are today? My path was less than ideal. I saw a lot of ineffective communication with my parents and did not learn the skills to be able to maneuver conflict very well as a child. I learned to keep my thoughts to myself when it did not fit with what was going on around me. Sometimes I would become adversarial and confrontational when I had to deliver a point of view that was bubbling up after stifling my voice for extended periods of time.

In the real world, needless to say, that did not bode well. I had to learn to communicate without shutting down or getting angry when I felt someone had a diametrically opposed point of view to my own. Fortunately, my early education, along with the field of psychotherapy, provided the ideal path to learn these skills.

## Early Communication Templates

Our early upbringing has a huge impact on the initial template of how we communicate. This preliminary pattern of safety and being able to use your words starts in your childhood. So, it is necessary to understand your style from the beginning of your life. Below are some reflective questions to get you started in the process.

### AUTHENTIC REFLECTING

Would you say that you were able to articulate your message quite clearly in childhood?

How would you describe communication within your family? How were issues dealt with?

Describe your father's communication style. Describe your mother's communication style. Who was the better communicator?

How would you describe your communication style as a child?

These early experiences are an important goalpost as it enables you to understand the things that you do to communicate well but, more importantly, what you do not do well. As I reflect on one of my early Leaders, I recall that she was strong, smart, articulate but she was often triggered outwardly when there was a differing point of view from her own. Unfortunately, while she was brilliant, she also allowed her emotions to impair her insight, which led to shortsighted decisions and nepotism in our department.

When she was triggered, she would raise her voice to an unprofessional level. She did not like to be challenged and was unable to heed the other team members' points of view, creating a lack of psychological safety. Her tirades would involve firing employees in the heat of the moment and rehiring them when she was calm.

Regrettably, the public sector afforded her a place where she could hide from her actions. She did not take responsibility for her behavior and would defer to the director to clean up her mess with staff after the fact. Needless to stay there was a lot of dissension and toxicity in that environment. This system provided a place of protection for this Leader. She only hired staff who would not stand up to her and if they did there were massive repercussions for their actions.

In considering my role in that situation, I used the buffer system, making use of my director to diffuse any concerns I had with the CEO. As a new Leader, I was eager to learn but I did so in a very controlled way. My director played a pivotal part in protection but really did a disservice to the system that needed to keep this CEO accountable. Unhappily, this CEO's shortcoming was never brought to the board so the unfairness and nepotism could not be rectified. It is Leaders like this that cause harm to not only new Leaders but all their staff.

This example is a bit extreme but demonstrates the misuse of power that happens more often than it should. Being an Authentic Leader means that one of your highest skills is relational transparency. This means that you need to look at yourself as objectively as possible. That being said, it is quite difficult to alter the subjective lens through which we see ourselves. It gets a bit easier as you task yourself in this area. Objective feedback becomes one of the core elements for growth in learning how to improve your communication style. It can be disconcerting to hear that you are not a good communicator, but try to take this as an opportunity to improve in this area. Even the best communicators can get better regardless of their competencies.

Think back to your early experiences in Leadership. Relational transparency is a good starting point for understanding the areas that come naturally to you and which ones need your focus.

In my early career the skill I had to learn was how to effectively deal with people who were more abrupt and autocratic in their approach. I was uncomfortable with this style of interaction and soon recognized that I would be triggered and go into a heightened state when interacting with this type of personality. I used reflection and tracking of my thoughts, feelings and body sensations to understand my internal space and adjust myself to more effectively converse when activated.

Relational transparency grows as deep reflection increases your personal Leadership growth. Reflection allows for amazing opportunities to grow and disrupts the flow of unconscious patterns that do not serve your evolution.

In your Leadership roles, are there times when you find it more difficult to be open? Reviewing these scenarios uncovers a lot of information that you may not be aware of on a conscious level. The old Leadership style of being autocratic has had its day. We must make room for the more effective Leader who is vulnerable and available and accomplishes so much more with less effort and time. This shoulder-to-shoulder leading allows others to get to know you, like you and trust you, which paves the way for an effective corporate culture.

I would like to share the story of one of the most Authentic Leaders I had the privilege of working with in the health and wellness arena.

## `CASE STUDY` *An Authentic Leader*

This Leader was one of the most amazing people I have ever known. He was so relatable that everyone wanted to work for him. He made you feel seen and heard. I had the privilege of being on this Leader's team for ten years.

What made him authentic was that he was always available to you, regardless of the circumstances that you were dealing with. He made you feel like you were special. He had a very playful, kind, caring way when he interacted with you. He got to know you as a person and understood what made you tick. He did this in a very smooth and fluid way and he would chat with you as a person while concurrently taking care of business. He was one of the best listeners I have experienced in my career. It was as if he could look inside you and know what was going on and then create solutions to consulting problems that made each problem seem small.

Even though there could be hundreds of thousands of dollars on the line, he always created a constructive space for problem solving. He was good-humored in his personality and he would greet you in such a warm way that it was a pleasure speaking with him even when things were not going well in business. He always dealt with you as a person first and created the space to make you feel like the business issues were of a secondary nature. He was collaborative and always wanted to understand your entire perspective on the problem prior to asserting his point of view to the solution. He never went to a resolution without a clear understanding of what you needed from him. His support was unconditional.

I can honestly say that annual performance evaluations were welcomed as he created such a positive experience, focusing always on what went well and then providing feedback on what was needed for your business growth. His scores in all the areas of Authentic Leadership would have quite positive rankings.

The way he approached the senior Leaders was the same manner in which he dealt with his team. He did not threaten anyone based on their position. He treated each person with the same value regardless of their position. His ability to join with people in the context of business was quite remarkable to watch. The level of acumen that he showed was exceptional.

My career success today is due in large part to this amazing man's capacity to mentor my skills to the point that I became the account executive who was assigned the more difficult portfolios. He had the gift of making each and everyone feel like they were the center of his attention when interacting with him.

Authentic Leaders are able to make people feel special; they have a magical touch. When these Leaders lead it is amazing to watch as the comportment with which they carry themselves is one of utmost poise and decorum.

## Be Intentional

With genuine relational transparency Leaders are able to line up their intentions with what motivates them. Most Leaders have the best of intentions but at times may come across in a vague manner, which waters down their message. This incongruence can create a space that disables employees' abilities to calculate your inner space and creates a lack of trust.

When employees are second guessing your intentions they become unfocused on the vital tasks at hand, impacting productivity. So, as a Leader, are your intentions clear? Clarity is key to keeping employees from wondering whether they can trust the Leader and, in turn, the organization. Consistency in your space as a Leader equals consistent actions in the others around you.

The best way to be steady as a new Leader is to state your intention up front as you get to know your team. If you are clear that you want to build openness and honesty on your team, others know what to expect from you. This sets a standard so that when there are inconsistencies team members can feel safe to approach the Leader.

## Transparency and the Pandemic

In the spring of 2020, the COVID-19 pandemic provided an opportunity to Authentic Heart Leaders to demonstrate their transparency to their staff. More than ever what was needed was the feeling of safety. At that time, it was an unprecedented notion that your care and concern would be the most important variable that your staff would remember.

Leaders' staff were in fear mode, like the rest of the world. A Leader's support needed to involve a certain amount of transparency to let staff know that you were experiencing a lot of the same concerns around friends, family, the new economy and growth. Your level of transparency created the space for connection that was needed at a time when we were learning to connect in a different way. One day we were at the office and the next we were learning how to run our businesses in conjunction with our personal lives.

Whether you had virtual teams prior to the pandemic or this was the first kick at the can, connection was needed on a much deeper level. Everyone was unsteady so Authentic Leaders needed to meet their teams where they were at and become the weather vane in the virtual room and the most relationally transparent they could possibly be. Through their internal space Leaders created a place of authenticity based on their internal reflection.

The pandemic space brought a lot of stressors to the forefront, such as work-life issues, disconnection from colleagues and fear of job loss. As Leaders your role was assisting your employees to find a new rhythm and pivot into a mode of accepting the situation as their new reality for an indeterminate time.

A dear friend of mine was becoming unhinged as the pandemic unfolded so she shifted and quickly put some new structure into her family routines to create a space where she felt in control. She started to demonstrate a Leadership role. She asked herself, "What can I do to create some flow for my family rather than staying in a zone of fear where I freeze up?" Each person was allotted a role in the new reality.

Both parents worked from home, one son was attending university and a grandson attended grade school. Additionally two elderly parents lived in their in-law apartment. Her husband ran his law practice in one area of the home, her teenage son did his university studies in her office and she helped her grandson with his school work. She decided that a daily family lunch that embraced the whole family, including her mother and step-father, was in order. She focused on what she valued. She got out of the fear zone and went into the learning zone.

During the pandemic Leaders had to demonstrate the learning zone to those around them. They needed to show their staff what they were learning about themselves virtually at that time. One of the most Authentic Leaders I know, Yves Doucet, President of Dovico,[19] held yoga classes for his staff from his home. I am not suggesting that we all have skills of this nature but the question was, "What can you do to let others see your learnings at this time?" How did you demonstrate that you were in the learning zone?

Perhaps you reached out like amazing Leader Scott Lyons did? President of Extend Communication Inc., he called each and every one of his 200 employees. Think of the unique ways you can reach out to let your employees know that you care and understand the space you are all in. Maybe you were innovative with your zoom meetings to ensure that you engaged all employees as much as you could through that time. Getting comfortable with the virtual realm was a skill that became vitally necessary then.

Initially, there was the settling period and we adapted to the onslaught of changes that came with the landscape of the pandemic but as the economy opened up there were different realities that became apparent. There were the realities of the economic implications of job loss, reintegrating teams or reestablishing and dealing with the fear that we carried forward of the virus returning for yet another wave. These were the new issues but there were also residual concerns that may not have been addressed prior to the onset of the pandemic.

So, we moved out of acceptance into a space of impatience and the reality of further uncertainty which brought about further fears. In consultations with companies, there was a concern trending around performance that employees were not performing at all at home. Initially there was the sense that everyone needed to band together to survive but as the dust settled issues were starting to rear up as employees were accepting the new reality of working from home.

On my podcast, Authentic Living with Roxanne, I interviewed Neil Cosby, an HR consultant, and he shared that his clients were reporting a rise in performance-related concerns since the commencement of the pandemic. The stressors of work/life balance were setting in along with the social isolation and disconnection from normal routines.

Pre-pandemic employees could compartmentalize their roles of employee or family member. During the pandemic there was a blurring of roles and employees were no longer able to parse out the time needed to maintain their mental and emotional health. This time period taught us much about ourselves as a species and became vital as we eventually started to resume our full lives again. We were in a heightened state of anxiety which may not dissipate for a while and, even when it does, there will always be a bit of low-grade fear of this uncertainty in our future.

When a Leader is able to demonstrate their intention to build trust on an ongoing basis, then their question of motive comes less into question. Any second guessing of intentions can create a corrosive element with relational transparency. I am not suggesting that your team second guesses your decision-making. If your actions appear out of alignment, it is best to have an open dialogue to deter your team from going underground to have discussions about your motives. These conversations may be tough but they are very necessary to work against the undercurrents of mistrust that can gain momentum if left unaddressed.

## Face Contention Head On

It is best to deal with contentious issues as they arise. It bodes well to increase communications more when you feel there is dissension. This is where your skills around reading the pulse of a room are very important. In meetings connect with your inner gut and if there appear to be issues swirling it is best to clarify what is going on. Reading the room and opening up dialogue gives those in the room a voice to share openly instead of driving the concerns and energy underground.

*Approach conflict with a positive attitude. Openness and positivity can create the real space for resolution.*

One of my first roles as a psychotherapist was joining a seasoned team of first responders with the police. This team had been working together for a long time. There was a distinct character to this team with a lot of strong personalities. As the newbie I was made aware of the various personalities and what roles they played on the team. I was fortunate to have been paired well with a partner who was respected by the team.

Our mode of communication was completed via a logbook. All current cases were documented in the log along with all action steps taken and the ones that needed to be taken by the oncoming shift. The logbook was a place where some of the difficult personalities would assert their dominance by crossing off actions they were unhappy with, negating the work another team member had done. As the newest member of the team I was often the target of abrasive communications as if it were a rite of passage.

As things became a bit unbearable I took my concerns to my team Leader who assured me that she would take care of my concerns. She did not have the skills to address these concerns so I lost faith in my ability to feel safe with this Leader. Her actions made me realize that she was scared of the abrasive team members so I started to mistrust her Leadership abilities.

The misalignment of this Leader's intention and actions created mistrust in her ability to lead. I had to seek out assistance from my peers to start asserting myself to gain a comfortable footing to do my job. Luckily I was strong enough to endure these behaviors; another may have left the situation due to the lack of support.

Relational transparency creates a space where your team can trust, build, take courageous action and thrive together.

 ## TASKS FOR AUTHENTICITY

When having conversations, practice looking at the person's face and body and use this as your guide for deeper understanding and connection.

Write an outline of a conversation with someone you are in conflict with. Stick to a couple of positive comments for the opening and then ask questions to seek to understand the other person's thoughts, feelings and perspective on the dispute.

## Chapter 7

# CONNECTION

## Leading from the Heart

Looking deep into your heart imparts a lot of answers to what is needed for your best Leadership version. I truly believe that the central element of being a great Leader is leading from the heart. So, where does this begin?

Quite literally it starts as soon as we are conceived. Our initial foray into the world creates the initial platform from which we build the rest of our lives. I could speculate that my parents' space was less than ideal but that I was born from a place of love. They had four children at a very young age. My early environment lacked safety and security which would have impacted my frame of reference.

Our world develops early and continues to be informed with each and every experience throughout our development. Exploring attachment enables us to decipher our core sense of self and its impact on our Leadership abilities. Let's begin our review with the four styles of attachment.

## The Four Styles of Attachment

British psychologist, psychiatrist and psychoanalyst John Bowlby pioneered work in attachment theory.[20] We will explore each style and how it may impact us and our capacity to interact with others. The styles are as follows:

1. secure,
2. anxious-preoccupied,
3. dismissive-avoidant and
4. fearful-unresolved.

### Secure

A secure attachment style is demonstrated by those possessing a positive view of self and a positive view of others.

Securely attached people tend to agree with the following statements.

- It is relatively easy for me to become emotionally close to others.
- I am comfortable depending on others and having others depend on me.
- I don't worry about being alone or others not accepting me.

This style of attachment usually results from a history of warm and responsive interactions with their attachments. Securely attached people tend to have positive views of themselves and their connections. They also tend to have positive views of their relationships. Often they report greater satisfaction and adjustment in their relationships than people with other attachment styles. Securely attached people feel comfortable both with intimacy and with independence.

Secure attachment and adaptive functioning are promoted by a caregiver who is emotionally available and appropriately responsive to their child's attachment behavior, as well as capable of regulating both their positive and negative emotion.

### Anxious-Preoccupied

An anxious-preoccupied attachment style is demonstrated by those possessing a negative view of self and a positive view of others.

People with anxious-preoccupied attachment tend to agree with the following statements.

- I want to be completely emotionally intimate with others, but I often find that others are reluctant to get as close as I would like.

- I am uncomfortable being without close relationships, but I sometimes worry that others don't value me as much as I value them.

People with this style of attachment seek high levels of intimacy, approval and responsiveness from their attachment figure. They sometimes value intimacy to such an extent that they become overly dependent on the attachment figure.

Compared with securely attached people, people who are anxious or preoccupied with attachment tend to have fewer positive views about themselves. They may feel a sense of anxiousness that only recedes when in contact with the attachment figure. They often doubt their worth as a person and blame themselves for the attachment figure's lack of responsiveness.

People who fall into this category may exhibit high levels of emotional expressiveness, emotional dysregulation, worry and impulsiveness in their relationships.

## Dismissive-Avoidant

A dismissive-avoidant attachment style is demonstrated by those possessing a positive view of self and a negative view of others.

People with a dismissive or avoidant style of attachment tend to agree with these statements.

- I am comfortable without close emotional relationships.
- It is important to me to feel independent and self-sufficient.
- I prefer not to depend on others or have others depend on me.

People with this attachment style desire a high level of independence. The desire for independence often appears as an attempt to avoid attachment altogether. They view themselves as self-sufficient and invulnerable to feelings associated with being closely connected to others.

They often deny needing close relationships. Some may even view close relationships as relatively unimportant. Not surprisingly, they seek less intimacy with attachments who they often view less positively than they view themselves.

Investigators commonly note the defensive character of this attachment style. People of the dismissive-avoidant attachment type tend to suppress and hide their feelings, and they tend to deal with rejection by distancing themselves from the sources of rejection (e.g., their attachments or relationships).

### *Fearful-Unresolved*

The fourth style's attachment patterns of behavior are demonstrated by those possessing an unstable or fluctuating view of self and others.

People with losses or other trauma, such as sexual abuse in childhood or adolescence, may often develop this type of attachment and tend to agree with the following statements.

- I am somewhat uncomfortable getting close to others.
- I want emotionally close relationships, but I find it difficult to completely trust others, or to depend on them.
- I sometimes worry that I will be hurt if I allow myself to become too close to other people.

They tend to feel uncomfortable with emotional closeness, and their mixed feelings sometimes are combined with unconscious, negative views about themselves and their attachments. They commonly view themselves as unworthy of responsiveness from their connections, and they don't trust the intentions of their attachments. Similar to the dismissive-avoidant attachment style, people with fearful-avoidant attachment seek less intimacy from their relationships and frequently suppress and deny their feelings. Because of this, they are much less comfortable expressing affection.

When you think of which style you present, you will get a sense of how you connect with others and, in turn, how your type may impact your Leadership style. While difficult to acknowledge which space you fall into, becoming aware of it is vitally important for your growth.

One of my blind spots was communicating effectively with someone who may have a diametrically opposed view from my own. I had to work through this internal process and come to a space where I could share with others, who were in a different place, room that was sincerely open so they did not feel shut down and could share. This was not an easy learning process but necessary for my growth. Getting into this kind of consciousness allows for real development as a Leader.

## Determining Your Attachment Style

I would like you to review the styles of attachment and determine which style you fit into. I would say that I fall into the anxious-preoccupied attachment category. In identifying your styles you can understand the gaps that may need focus to facilitate your growth. Let's review each style and discuss some of the concerns using Figure 5.

*Figure 5*

**IDENTIFYING YOUR ATTACHMENT STYLE**

| Attachment Type | Self-Talk | Impact on Relationship | Area of Focus | Steps to Focus on |
|---|---|---|---|---|
| Secure | You have the skills to figure things out. You have negative and positive thoughts. It is your job to focus on the positive one. | You have amazing connections in your life. You have different connections for the varying needs in your life. | You are always striving to improve yourself and welcome feedback from others. | You challenge yourself to understand others different from you. You try to keep your thoughts and feelings straight by getting them out of yourself with pen and paper. |

| Attachment Type | Self-Talk | Impact on Relationship | Area of Focus | Steps to Focus on |
|---|---|---|---|---|
| Secure (continued) | You are not defined by your thoughts.<br><br>This too will pass. | You feel so fortunate that you can share openly with people close to you.<br><br>Your support system is always available; it is up to you to reach out when you need them. | You are able to be vulnerable when needed, to let others know that you are available.<br><br>You check in with yourself when stressed to ensure that you are not cut off from others long-term. | Self-care is important so you can keep an internal pulse on yourself.<br><br>Taking microbreaks helps level you on an ongoing basis.<br><br>Understanding others around you is a key strategy that you use in all areas of your life. |
| Anxious-Preoccupied | You sometimes feel like others fall short of your expectations as you go above and beyond in everything you do.<br><br>You worry at times that you might smother others when you feel anxious about losing connection with them.<br><br>Sometimes you do too much when you feel unsteady in an interaction with others. | Sometimes you feel that others are too distant in your interactions with them.<br><br>You feel like you want to experience a deep sense of connection to others, maybe more than others want.<br><br>You often worry that you do not do enough to gain acceptance by others. | Often you gauge how you are doing from others' feedback.<br><br>You share with others but are often guarded for fear of not being good enough.<br><br>You have to work on being more open with others and sharing the real you versus a contrived version of yourself. | You should learn how to listen to your negative thoughts and shift them to positive ones.<br><br>Understanding your triggering cues and learning effective ways to stay present in the situation is necessary.<br><br>You need to enhance your ability to focus on your achievements and defocus on feedback that is invalid. |

| Attachment Type | Self-Talk | Impact on Relationship | Area of Focus | Steps to Focus on |
|---|---|---|---|---|
| **Anxious-Preoccupied** (continued) | | Often you have trouble leaving positions as you do not want to break a connection with others, even though the move is better for you.<br><br>You seek validation from others that you are doing a good job. | You have to work on focusing on your positives and being grounded in who you are and what you have accomplished. | Recognizing the emotional part of yourself helps enhance your capacity to lead from a space of realness and being present. |
| **Dismissive-Avoidant** | Closeness in relationships is overrated.<br><br>Relying on yourself makes you feel good; not so much when you rely on others.<br><br>Being self-sufficient is the way you were brought up.<br><br>You don't understand others who let people get close so easily. | You're not sure when your connections are healthy.<br><br>You feel that being distant is best in a relationship.<br><br>Sharing too much is difficult for you.<br><br>Controlling what others know about you is vital. | It is important that you work on being more reliant on others.<br><br>You need to take small steps to allow others into your space, a bit at a time.<br><br>You must learn the difference between being hyper-vigilant and independent. | Journaling helps you understand what you do to guard yourself in relation to others.<br><br>You can better appreciate true connection in your-self by testing out the space with oth-ers you are close to in your personal life.<br><br>You want to explore all types of feelings with someone you trust or someone with expertise, such as a coach. |

| Attachment Type | Self-Talk | Impact on Relationship | Area of Focus | Steps to Focus on |
|---|---|---|---|---|
| Dismissive-Avoidant (continued) | | | Being connected to others does not mean you will lose your identity. | |
| Fearful-Unresolved | You don't really think that others have your best interests at heart.<br><br>Even though you have good people in your life they do not see the whole you.<br><br>You are always on guard waiting for the other shoe to drop. | You are fearful of being close to others.<br><br>You feel that being alone is better than allowing others in.<br><br>Others are always in it for their own self-interest.<br><br>You have trouble with the concept of trust. | Your safety and security are key.<br><br>You prefer to work alone even though working together with others may be a benefit.<br><br>You tend to work too much in order to ensure that you don't need others to assist you.<br><br>You cannot rely on others. | You must focus on understanding what safety and security means to you.<br><br>You need to gauge your internal sense of trust and develop it within yourself to start to notice it in others.<br><br>You tend to take small steps to let others in a bit at a time.<br><br>You use meditation to slow yourself and understand how you think, feel and act when there is trust and come in contact with what you expect of others. |

## Attachment Styles and Impact on Leadership

As a Leader, you will fluctuate from scenario to scenario, but ultimately want to work toward secure attachment, creating the base for the best version of yourself. In reviewing each style you will be able to decipher your fit.

## AUTHENTIC REFLECTING

When looking at yourself with reference to the four attachment styles, are you gentle and kind to yourself or intolerant?

What is the space within your internal world?

Once you are able to classify yourself, this is the starting point to work from and the implications for your Leadership development. When you are able to understand this space, you are creating a sacred place of growth that can be bestowed onto others in the leadership journey.

Ideally the securely attached style is the space where all Leaders should attempt to sit most often. However, sometimes leaders may waver, due to a new situation, an unidentified trigger or any multitude of reasons that come up in life. The good news is that continually being connected to your Leadership style allows you to make corrections to your path when you deviate, so you can make the soundest decisions more often than not.

From a securely connected space, you will have goals and aspirations with a clear path of what it takes to achieve those goals. If there is deviation from attainment of those goals, a securely attached Leader will create gentleness and kindness when things go off course.

The space of kindness and gentleness within authentic Leaders is needed so that, in turn, they can empower that space when obstacles appear on the track. This is key to grasp in order to lead from the heart. As the Leader fills up from a heart-centered space, it impacts the interactional space with others through osmosis.

*Authentic Leadership takes skills to show emotion, vulnerability and connection with employees in a natural and consistent way.*

### *Anxious-Preoccupied Leader*

The anxious pre-occupied style most resonates with my upbringing. As a Leader I worked at gaining validation within myself so it did not impact my ability to lead effectively. This skill deficit was challenged early in my career as a team Leader at a hospital clinic. My ability to ground internally created the space of safety needed to develop a level of trust, previously not experienced by this team due to previous poor Leadership.

If you can relate, reflect on what is needed to create safety for your employees. Are you looking for unrealistic levels of closeness with your team due to your style? What needs to happen to find the right balance between being liked versus respected? As a Leader it was nice to be liked at times, but I soon realized being respected was far more worthy.

## AUTHENTIC REFLECTING

Are you overly focused on being liked by your team members?

Do you find that you want an inordinately high level of intimacy with your team?

Do you have an overly negative view of yourself as a Leader?

Do you find that you are overly emotional when responding to team members?

Do you find it difficult to regulate your emotions if there is conflict on your team?

Do you find that your mood is dictated by what is going on with your direct reports?

Do you find you are less positive with yourself if there are conflicts on your team?

Do you take responsibility for your team members' behavior even when it is not warranted?

What is your general view of relationships on your team?

Overall, if you have responded "yes" to most of these questions, you would fall in the category of anxiously attached Leadership. Working on internally validating oneself as a leader creates the growth necessary to enhance your Leadership skills.

### Dismissive-Avoidant Leader

The dismissive-avoidant style views themselves as positive and the world around them as negative. They see real value in not being dependent on others.

How might this style play out in your Leadership? If you are not showing any vulnerability what space does that create for vulnerability in others around you. This desire to show that you do not need attachment to others can really generate distance on a team.

In one of my corporate roles, a recent merger had taken place. There was a lot of uncertainty and stress related to amalgamating two systems. My entire team was under duress as an inordinate number of changes were occurring. I went from having a full-time assistant to a third of an assistant's time along with being assigned one of the largest accounts in the company. At this time, more than ever I needed additional support from my senior VP. I was in a constant state of hyperarousal and felt like there was not much I could do right.

My senior VP definitely fit the dismissive-avoidant style. She did not show her vulnerability and she managed her stress by micromanaging the team. This ineffective Leadership style further created dissension on the team and eventually everyone was looking for other opportunities. I was offered a severance package after a brutal year of enduring this environment. I went from being one of the best on the team to being told "You are no longer a fit to the corporate objective of the new merger."

The senior Leader faded off into the background as HR took over discussing my package. Needless to say I received multiple phone calls from colleagues asking what steps I had taken to get out of my situation as they wanted to leave as well. About a year later that senior VP revealed that she had to take a short-term leave right after my departure due to stress.

In retrospect, had she shown her vulnerability, the team would have felt supported. When vulnerability is lacking there is dissension on teams and this inevitably leads to a lack of trust.

## AUTHENTIC REFLECTING

When you are having a difficult time do you push members of your team away?

Would your team members say that they can rely on you when they are having a tough time?

How do you let others around you know when you are having a tough time?

Would you say that you would be perceived as hyper-independent even when it is obvious that you need support?

When your team is going through a hard time, how do you support them?

Reflect on the last time you dealt with a difficult situation. How did you garner support from others around you?

Would you say that you have trouble showing your vulnerability with others?

If your team members were asked if you were approachable during a crisis, what do you think they would say?

Do you view needing intimacy in relationships as a weakness or a strength?

If you find that when you answer these questions you resonate with this style, then it makes sense to understand yourself and what needs to be addressed to enhance your skill with this style.

### *Fearful-Unresolved Leader*

A fearful-unresolved Leader is an individual who would have endured trauma in childhood or adolescence. This style views the world as not a safe place and finds it difficult to trust people. People that have issues of this nature, work arduously to not connect with others. This individual may be one of the best workers but struggles to connect to others on projects. As a Leader with this style it is important that you work to resolve the old issues of harm so you can connect to others. Mistrust will be perpetuated if you work in isolation. If, as a Leader, you relate to this style, there would be a lot of factors that you need to think about and deal with.

## AUTHENTIC REFLECTING

Do you find it difficult to trust regardless of who people are?

Do you find it difficult to get close to others on your team, although you want to get close to them?

Do you honestly believe that others cannot be trusted, even though your team members have never given you reason to mistrust them?

Think of the last time that you were able to trust one of your team members. Reflect on what it took for you to trust them.

Do you find that it is difficult for you to express your emotions? Do you generally suppress your emotions?

Do you usually believe that your team members do not have your best interests in mind?

Reviewing and reflecting on your attachment style really gives you a sense of what your heart shares with you when you come into a relationship with others. It is difficult to look at this space as a Leader but reflection allows an objective space for growth.

Based on the various attachment styles you can see how your role on a team could present many opportunities for misinterpretation of information. Most teams have a combination of styles but when the Leader connects to their style and leads from their heart, it creates a space of safety for the team to function.

If you are unaware of the deficits of your style, then naturally you will bump up against other styles quite often. By continually adapting your style to come as close as possible to a securely attached Leadership style, your team will have a secure landing pad from which they can thrive and grow. Really the gift that you give yourself is also one that you give others around you. Being fully present and leading from your heart will outweigh any metrics in a business plan.

## Connecting with Individuals and the Team

Each and every one of your team members needs to feel safe with you at any given time. That being said, certain foundational elements need to be established with each person individually and then collectively as a team.

Each person has to feel a sense of connection to you. This is the core foundational element of trust. If each team member gets to know you as a person then this falls naturally into place.

*Gauge how authentic you are as a Leader by aligning what you think, say and do.*

Leaders frequently focus on skills that are tactical and results driven. While quite necessary, alone they are not powerful unless coupled with team cohesion. It is the connection to the Leader that is the veritable glue within a team. Think of trust and whether it exists on your team. When you enter a room, does the energy or conversation change because you have entered the room?

Lack of trust takes many forms. Typically you may see unmet deadlines, conflict or a general lack of enthusiasm on the team. Knowing the level of trust that exists is the starting point to understanding what you need to make change as a Leader.

## *Technique*

Measuring trust is something that you can do starting from today.

Run through each team member and assign a level of trust that you feel exists between you and that individual. This is a reflective space that allows you to get an image of where things are at in that moment in time.

You want to explore this space to determine how you demonstrate caring and love for yourself. Next, ask yourself how this space plays out in your day-to-day interactions with everyone.

If you think this action is too warm and fuzzy, then think again. It is an important part of leading from the heart in an authentic way.

## AUTHENTIC REFLECTING

When you are not feeling good internally, what do you do to take care of yourself emotionally?

When you are not feeling well emotionally, what kind of support do you need from others? How do you elicit what you need from others in your life?

How do you care for your physical body? Exercise? Sleep? Nutrition?

What do you do to manage your thoughts on a routine basis?

What signals to you that you are getting run down emotionally, psychologically, biologically and spiritually?

What are the relationships in your life that bring you joy?

How do you create space to ensure that you replenish yourself on a routine basis?

How do you set limits with others to ensure that you maintain homeostatic balance at work and at home?

How would you define self-love?

Who are the support systems in your life? Who mentors you? Who makes you laugh? Who do you play with?

### Fullness Versus Depletion

By constructing your space of self-love and developing rituals, you will be able to meet the needs of others from a place of fullness versus one of depletion. In understanding your attachment style you are able to create an internal window that optimizes your capacity in all areas of life, not just Leadership. Upon reflection on my style, I can sometimes be tough on myself so I keep my eyes on my distortions and engage in strategies that keeps this gap in check.

If you are disconnected from this space you are less able to have an objective view of others and circumstances around you and this can be detrimental to your teams. Lack of trust takes its toll on teams. To validate this idea, I performed an observational experiment when I visited companies to roll out their health and wellness strategies.

On my first visit to the company, I surveyed the first line of reception. I could often decipher the tempo of the space within the company. I noticed the energy of reception and how they interfaced with the public. Occasionally I would be ignored for a lengthy period of time and in other instances I was engaged in a connected way.

Trust and kindness are unconscious currency. If it begins at the senior level, it trickles down to each and every employee and will impact the energy of your company, starting with an area as inconspicuous as reception.

Once you have figured out what skills you need to nurture, based on your attachment style, then the next logical step is to think how you will show up as a Leader. This is the "why" of Leadership.

## Your Leadership Why

Your "why" is where I believe your core foundational elements of who you are as a person lay.

The principal fundamentals of Starbuck's Leadership were integrity, hard work and creating an atmosphere that was like having coffee in the comfort of your living room. Starbuck's owner saw his father struggle to make a living but did not recognize that he had gleaned these values from these lessons. Upon deeper reflection he was able to parse out what was valuable from his father's Leadership – integrity, trust and hard work. He did not realize the significant influence his father had on the foundational elements to his own Leadership.

It is important to reflect on your why of Leadership. What are the main features that drive you to be the best Leader that you can possibly be? This becomes the main navigation system from which you make decisions – big and small – and can always use to realign yourself when Leadership becomes difficult.

## CASE STUDY  *My Why*

My Leadership why is encapsulated in a combination of many qualities.

I always want to ensure that everyone in my space has an equal opportunity to use their voice along with being faithful to my strong work ethic. These qualities are based on values that are important to my life story.

The attribute of hard work came from my father, who worked his way up in business from starting out as the child of cane farmers, and my mother, who cared for six children at quite a young age. My father's efforts moved him up the ranks from sales to executive Leadership. Without any formal education, he used his natural skills and ability to lead others. He worked very hard to afford a lifestyle that permitted my mother to stay at home and care for the family. My mother ran a tight ship and took care of the emotional and physical needs of the entire household. She never missed an event related to my school or extra-curricular activities.

The other value – equally as important – is that of voice. At a young age I recognized that women did not have as much say as men did. Quite early on I wanted to ensure that I and other girls would have an equal right to be heard on issues. At times the ability, even though encouraged in my education, could be absent at home. I needed to ensure that I had a voice but, equally important, that voice had to be authentic.

I found that in order to be heard you needed to create a space that allowed you to shine through. In order to develop my voice getting an education was a given, and this attitude was reflected throughout my culture and consistently mirrored within my family. Education was power. This was something my parents afforded their children with the intention of breaking the cycle and creating the power needed to survive and gain status in the world.

When I think back on the beginnings of my family, they were indentured laborers from India and the Middle East. When I was just in primary school I remember my mother telling me that I was going to university and this is something that I repeated to my son when he was also quite young. I realize the importance of this legacy now, as an adult recalling my ancestral beginnings.

Recently, I watched a five-part series on the conditions and realities of what my ancestors endured to make the trip from India and the Middle East to settle in Trinidad. It helped me understand the core fundamentals of my parents but it also gave me a reflective lens through which to view my parents' values based, in part, on their pasts. Hard work and education were drilled into me at an early age but now, as an adult, I understand this from a different space.

My father was accepted to law school and even though his parents wanted him to go and would have sacrificed for him to do so, he decided to become a legal clerk and help his parents educate his four younger siblings. My mother's family were merchants and a bit more privileged but she became a mother at the young age of eighteen and devoted her life to raising her six children.

My values of Leadership became imbued in me at an early age.

So, what are the fundamental core values of your Leadership? Your why becomes the GPS that guides your Leadership even when things are lonely and difficult. This becomes a fundamental space where you can retreat to and recalibrate your Leadership dilemmas.

It is immensely important to reflect on your Leadership story. Writing about your Leadership story provides a deeper understanding of core values and your path. Here are some reflective questions to start the process.

## AUTHENTIC REFLECTING

What are the core fundamental values of your Leadership style?

When you think of your values, what is the story of these values?

Who were the primary influencers of those values?

How did your upbringing influence those values?

How do your beliefs, values and assumptions play out in your Leadership style?

How do your core values influence your decision-making as a Leader?

Reflect on ethical dilemmas in your Leadership roles that may have impacted you in detrimental ways.

When have your values been in alignment with your Leadership story or when not?

What lessons have you learned along your Leadership path that have heightened your values and alignment?

Are there valuable lessons that you learned as a new Leader that continue to impact your Leadership story?

When reflecting back on my early Leadership posts, there were many times when these positions did not correlate with my core Leadership values. When the misalignments were significant, my time in these roles was very stressful and I second guessed my capacity to lead.

One of the most important lessons that I learned was how the alignment of my values was critical to leading authentically. That being said, freshly out of graduate school I thought less about these concerns and focused on the task at hand – starting my career and earning a living.

As part of my growth process I ascertained very early what I needed to not only survive but to thrive in certain environments. Lack of fit means making tough decisions which may ultimately mean leaving the situation or, minimally, ensuring that your next choice has the core elements to allow you to lead from an authentic space.

## Connecting for Your Own Good

Leading from the heart is imperative not just to your well-being but also for the benefit of all those who surround you. Some studies from the HeartMath Institute[21] show the importance of leading from this space, including empirical evidence that it impacts metrics associated with better overall heath. Some of the findings are quite astounding.

They found hypertensive employees at Hewlett Packard experienced better outcomes (as much as 28% decrease in diastolic and systolic blood pressure).[22] The Reform Church of America reduced heart care costs as much as $585 per participant,[23] as well as decreases in symptoms in the areas of PTSD, pain reduction and ADHD. Additionally, the HeartMath Institute has been doing research around the importance of aligning breathing to synchronize with the energetic fields that surrounds us.

HeartMath's concept is based on the fact that when your heart beats at the correct rate of variability, the alignment that is needed for your entire system to function better is created. The largest health-related costs in North America are linked to cardio-vascular disease. The HeartMath Institute looks at the impact of heart rate variability (HRV) on overall health. In medical circles blood pressure is the focus, but it is really less significant than our HRV. Alignment is key. When we are in a relaxed state our body is in tune with what it needs in order to flow naturally and all our organs are aligned the way they need to.

When there is a lack of alignment of the heart, mind and emotions, there is a disruption of the flow needed for optimal functioning of your body. Research has shown that your heart beats at a rate of .01 Hertz when it is fully aligned. This is the same frequency at which the earth vibrates naturally. This is fascinating. When you are in alignment with your body, its messengers in its natural state send messages to your heart or creates heart coherence, which makes us resonate at a level that is best for us to function.

If Leaders are able to impact their internal systems, then they can and will impact the energy around them, approximately a three-meter circumference. This requires them to take their self-awareness to a much deeper level where they can impact their overall health and that of others around them.

### Self-Care

Back in Chapter 4 we discussed the dysregulation that occurs when you are triggered by ongoing stressful events. Your body naturally reacts to protect you from threat by going into the fight, flight or freeze response.

If stress is a state that is normal throughout your day then the body goes from triggering to activating the sympathetic nervous system over and over again, which dysregulates every system in your body, impacting the existing health conditions within your company. When organizations look at the analysis of their short-term and long-term disability claims, this phenomenon is evident. As a Leader, you can look at what is going on within your environment through the analysis of these claims and make an impact, starting with the space that you create within yourself.

*Authentic Leadership is all encompassing – listen to your body, it has the clues for growth ahead of your thoughts.*

The pandemic of 2020-22 provided a good example. What did your team need from you through that time? They needed to know that you were living in an authentic way. They needed compassion, kindness, caring, structure and open dialogue, reassuring them that everyone was in it together. They needed to know that you could effectively role model coping with fear, volatility and panic, all the normal feelings that everyone was experiencing at that time.

So, first you want to ask yourself, "How am I doing? You need to go into your internal work and start to take stock of what is really going on for you. This is a time where being real is being dictated to you. If you have struggled with being real, a situation like a pandemic will mean that you will need to pivot and figure out how to create this space immediately.

So, here you are. What are you going to do to deal with your mindset? What are your pressures right now? Is your family at home with you? What is your mindset in this new state? Some reflective questions will assist you with a plan of action.

## AUTHENTIC REFLECTING

What activities do you do on a daily basis to take care of yourself?

What steps do you take to manage your mindset?

Reflect on your nutrition, water intake, overall physical well-being.

Do you exercise? If so, how many times a week?

Do you have a sleep routine? How many hours do you sleep?

Who is your support system? Please identify. What role does each person play in your world?

How do connect with your spouse and/or children on a daily basis?

What makes you laugh daily?

Spending this time with these questions will create a space within you that you will be able to utilize through all uncertain times and start your space of leading authentically. If this is the first time looking at yourself from this self-care perspective, there will be definite gaps but it is a beginning point that will equip you with some skills to start steering the ship in this new direction. Without your ability to anchor and take care of yourself, it becomes difficult to demonstrate care for others.

The need to feel safety from Leadership was important in the past but now has become a non-negotiable. Gone are the days when Leaders lead without demonstrating their truth. Authentic Leadership will guide you and your teams to the other side of this uncertainty. Whether during a time of pandemic or not, your teams will gain a sense of what you are made of and in that environment you will be well equipped, regardless of what comes knocking.

Your regulated HRV will impact those on your senior Leadership teams and will create a cascade effect to middle management, then to front-line employees and finally to the customer. In my tenure as a corporate consultant I had a front-row seat to senior managers who were not attuned to their heart space.

One particular senior Leader was known for getting things done but created a chaotic environment wherever he went in the organization. He ran the sales department for a financial institution and kept the company at the top tier of the industry. However the tirades his teams were exposed to endure when things were not going well were legendary. He was unliked by most of his staff except for his inner circle who he protected with fierceness.

Within the company he was often referred to in the most derogatory terms, but the board did not address the ongoing concerns that were brought to the table due to the level of performance that this senior Leader achieved year over year. He mostly concerned himself with the return on investment and growth of the organization only from a bottom-line perspective. He was clearly disconnected from what was in the best interest of his employees and would ridicule his staff. Eventually, to save their health and happiness a lot of the team members changed departments and some even went over to the competitors.

This senior Leader drove himself at such a high level that he had to take an abrupt sick leave because he suffered a heart attack. He returned to the same environment in a short time and carried on with the same behavior. This Leader is an example of someone who was disconnected from his heart and in turn created an energy that burnt out his staff, impacted is own health and created turn over, although he still made the numbers, on which this company was most focused.

To this organization, the numbers mattered most and people were not taken into account of the bigger picture. In the short term, to an uneducated eye, this situation was not an issue but long-term metrics would state otherwise.

The HeartMath Institute would be able to look at this situation and measure how the negative energy created by this Leader impacted the health concerns and, in turn, the hard bottom-line numbers for this company.

## Coherence

The organization described in the story in the section above would be an example of what Rollin McCraty,[24] would describe as a company that was struggling with personal and social coherence.

From the space of self-regulation, we are able to stay grounded within ourselves, creating a space where we can relate to others on a consistent basis, regardless of the circumstances surrounding us, in order to better create improved families, schools, and communities, which can have a global impact. If Leaders are able to tune into this space, then the affect will be priceless in every system of your life. There would be more tolerance and harmony, and less frustration, anxiety, worry and irritation. That being said, your left brain is probably wondering how can this be possible. The data now exists to quantify the information of HRV – it's coherence.

When there is the alignment of the heart, mind and emotions, this creates a mental clarity that impacts your ability to function optimally. In shifting the heart to a more resilient mindset, you create and maintain behavioral changes. How would this impact your peers, employees and everyone around your space? When using the space of personal regulation, then social regulation is possible and this positive impact travels far and wide with each system that surrounds you.

In shifting into a connected coherent state, there is the decrease in frustration, anxiety, worry and irritation. By focusing on one breath, you can access feelings of appreciation, gratitude and kindness and you'll experience an immediate change in attitudes, emotions and intentions. The concept that the heart is more important as a neural messenger to the brain than the brain is to the heart is a newer model to the field of science. This signal from the heart to the brain is the main regulator of our internal hormonal balance.

The vagus nerve is the information super-highway between our internal and external worlds. When there is alignment with the vagus system, there is an ability to engage the parasympathetic nervous system, which creates energy, replenishment and autonomic balance. This condition is easily achieved with proper inhalation, moving us from a fight or flight state to one of relaxation. The breath creates the space of coherence needed for balance.

Is coherence different from relaxation? In fact there is a huge difference. Coherence produces a deeper, internal synchronization compared to relaxation. An example of ultimate relaxation is taking a nap, but coherence is about having a higher HRV, which generates harmonization and enables your capacity to center and optimize cognitive functioning.

## AUTHENTIC REFLECTING

During the day, how often are you aware of what is happening physiologically to your body?

How often might you be triggered by stressful situations throughout the day?

Do you take time daily to focus on your sensory space and become present to all senses?

Are you aware of the stressors in your day that may dysregulate you?

What grounding strategies do you use throughout the day to support yourself?

What cues do you recognize biologically, psychologically, emotionally or socially that you are stressed?

Do you have your day mapped out so you have energy at the end of your day to enjoy the other parts of your life?

When you are dysregulated, how does your behavior impact others around you?

How might others recognize the difference in your behavior towards them when you are dysregulated?

What strategies do you use to pivot out of a dysregulated state that are not helpful to your well-being?

Is it possible to implement short quick bits to your day that allow you to connect internally to safeguard your well-being?

From the answers above you will get a sense of how in tune you are with your internal space. If you recognize that you are often in a dysregulated state, there are several breathing exercises that may be helpful for you to begin implementing throughout your day.

### Breathing Strategies to Cope with Dysregulation

These tactics can be performed throughout your day, like taking a coffee break.

Use your phone to remind you to perform these three types of breathing. I often share this strategy with senior Leaders who use a favorite song as their alarm reminder to implement the breath.

1. **Four-Round Breathing:** This should be done for a round of ten breaths, three times a day. Find a comfortable spot in a chair and plant your feet firmly on the ground. If possible close your eyes, but it is not necessary. Then, through your nose, take four short inhales, then exhale four quick breaths. Do this ten times. As suggested, you can do this exercise two or three times a day. This is a staple breathing exercise that should be used often and should come naturally after a while.

2. **Four Inhale/Eight Exhale Breathing:** This exercise should also be done as needed throughout the day. Find a place where you are able to sit with your back straight and close your eyes if possible. Inhale for a count of four and then exhale for eight. This form of breathing will tap into the parasympathetic nervous system, the state that brings calm to the body. As suggested you should do this breathing technique several times throughout the day, but may not be needed as often as the four-round breathing. However, when anxiety or irritability arise, it is a good idea to use this method to regulate the central nervous system.

3. **Fire Breathing:** This breathing is practiced less often than the other two. Use it when you realize that you are depleted or on the road to depletion. This method is a bit different from the

other two and it can look a little silly, but it gives the body the detox it needs from the stressors of depletion. Find a quiet spot and sit with your back straight. Take a deep breath in. Exhale through your nose, using short bursts from the lower abdomen — you will see movement in your abdomen. It sounds a bit like a dog panting. Try to exhale 20 bursts for every inhalation. It may not be possible at first, but keep practicing.

These breathing techniques applied throughout the day will regulate your HRV and create the homeostatic balance needed to regulate your central nervous system all day. It is difficult to believe that we need to learn how to breathe but it is vitally important to recognize that the body stores all memories, whether good or bad. When your system is taxed, the unconscious mind goes into protection mode unbeknownst to you. This protection is not detrimental in the short term but it can have dangerous implications to your long-term health.

### The Heart Lock Method for Coping

If you are able to access your system where you are connected to your heart, this will put you more in alignment with your internal space. Often when you start your day you get disconnected with a vital space within yourself. There are a lot of different exercises that will help you access the heart but the HeartMath Institute has quick methods that are conducive to use during your busy days.

The Heart Lock Method enables you to connect to that space every quickly. This can be done within minutes when using one of the breathing techniques (described above) by adding a second part — meditate so you connect to your heart and think of a moment or moments that you are most grateful for. I know that we all have a lot of things we are grateful for but accessing these memories puts your entire system into a blissful state.

One of my most precious memories was the moment my son was born and he was put onto my chest in the hospital. This recollection brings an instant space of gratefulness that accesses a deep part of my heart. This is a practice that is easy and can be performed as often as possible through your day. This connection will allow your system the space to recalibrate your heart and, in turn, all your organization from the dysregulated state of the sympathetic nervous system to the parasympathetic system of relaxation.

The more often Leaders are connected to themselves, the more able they are to influence the space in others in their environment. Your energy will permeate your space and then will regulate the emotions of others around you.

 ## TASKS FOR AUTHENTICITY

Think of the last time there was an opportunity to share with your employees. What did you do? How do you feel about the level of sharing?

Once a week, jot down how aligned you are in heart, mind and emotions and decide what needs more focus.

Scan your body daily and listen to what the emotions in your body are whispering to you.

# Chapter 8

# RECOGNITION

Recognition has a special place in all our lives. I often think of the roles that I have played in my life and what the value of being recognized meant to me and my development and growth.

When relating recognition to the other four elements of Authentic Heart Leadership it is important to follow the process from an internal frame to one of intentionality when acknowledging others. Initially, starting from an internal space of introspection affords the Leader the space to realize what is needed to employ their knowledge in practical, didactic application with others. A connected Leader is able to use their aerial view to create the appreciation needed that serves all versus a few.

Your relationship with recognition has a deep-rooted space.

In my family of six there was the first child – the golden child special just because – then the second child, who struggled to find importance out of the shadow of the golden child, the third was special being the only boy and then came me. The role that I garnered was one of connector. And my sister followed. She flayed to find her magic power until she found creativity. Finally, the last child, like the first, was special because of the unique place of being the baby.

As a family therapist we identify and honor the role and space that each child plays and the extent to which each person plays in eking out their specialness. Recognition is something that we all want in some way or form and it becomes important that we understand ourselves and then create a platform for others who also want to be acknowledged.

## Reciprocity

This mutual need for recognition is glaringly obvious when we are conversing with someone. When you have the skill to focus the conversation on the other person, it is interesting to see the passion that emerges as the discussion becomes about them.

Most of us love talking about our lives, not in an egocentric way but we get passionate about our lives and want to share. When having conversations with others, most will lose interest if there is not a reciprocity in the dialogue after a certain period of time. Initially, we may all intently listen, but eventually we become disenchanted.

*Success in communication means you are getting better with each successful conversation.*

As a Leader how are you demonstrating that you are really listening with the intention of learning a bit more about the other person, as opposed to meeting with them for a means to an end. If your exchanges tend to have a focus on a sole business purpose, you are working at cross-purposes to connection. The ability to understand what someone needs starts with a simple conversation and eventually the cumulative impact provides an aerial view of the aggregate needs of your employees as a whole. It allows a window into the culture of your team and, ultimately, what is needed for validation.

## Know Your People

Who are your staff? This is the main question. And how do you let them know that they are valued, based on the amazing things they accomplish year over year for your company?

The point is not to look at compensation as a metric but, rather, determining the values that are most important in your company. You want to ensure that the rewards and recognition awards are based on those values. You want to make certain that the performance metrics are centered on these ideals to create the foundation to which you need to adhere. Again, as I think of all the clients that I work with who are in relationships in any capacity, what is most important is that they are seen. If people are rewarded on all the elements of what the company values this creates a synergy that allows all employees to work towards compensation based on who they are.

In my corporate career, compensation was most often strictly financial and the stars of the organization were a subset of the company that performed the best in bringing in new business. Meanwhile, there were core parts of the business performing fundamental tasks that made the sales team shine. These essential people were not rewarded for all the hard work that they accomplished behind the scenes, but year after year the bonuses got bigger for the "stars" and so did the kudos from the Leadership team. This is like going back to the family system example. There will always be the star and the baby and all the others, regardless of what they did, could not get the limelight.

Companies and teams should be aware of this reality and work to ensure that all parts of the system get what they need to feel valuable. If everyone sees that each and every part of the system gets recognized for their efforts, regardless of the pecking order, then space is created for one and all to work to their optimum level of productivity.

## Awarding Credit

As a Leader it is important to work out your story of how you like to be recognized and this creates the space and understanding on what that means to you. Then in your space, you will gain insights into what others may need, even if they are diametrically opposed to you.

## CASE STUDY *Opposing Needs*

The IT department at this company was regarded as the backbone because they created delivery for all the services to the customers in a seamless way. They were the ones who would work arduously to achieve tasks that were generally thought to be close to impossible. The team was led by an amazing man who was good at what he did but he lacked much skill in the area of recognition.

His team was regularly under a lot of pressure as was he. He was cordial, kind and connected but he did not give feedback and recognition to the members of his team. He worked them tirelessly. They often put in sixteen-hour days to complete a product launch or deal with glitches that could cost the company hundreds of thousands of dollars if not addressed. This Leader found it difficult to savor the successes as there was always a new initiative coming around the bend. The team was frequently recognized quickly for a new product launch and then the pressure would be on yet again.

This Leader was the type of person who drove himself at a high level and he did not need a lot of feedback on his accomplishments. He was completely unaware that his style was impacting his team. The C-Suite had an expectation that allowed no room for errors and this SVP worked in alignment with their needs, repeatedly pushing his team to dire levels.

The morale on his team was low and while he would see this situation, he did not stop to understand the needs of the team. He worked from his internal space that an accomplished goal was something he enjoyed quietly but he did not know what his team required. This dedicated team continued to deliver but over time there was a necessity for more. The Leader needed to use his self-awareness to understand his space of recognition and how it may be diametrically opposed to others on his team. He did not connect that his team receiving rewards was a must to create the cohesiveness required for the continued level of achievement.

Unfortunately, with time a lot of the IT team was lost to competitors and the team that was left were visibly not in a good space. Without the core elements of understanding how his style of his Leadership disconnected him from his team, this Leader lost his valuable human capital.

As I reflect on my story of what I needed to be recognized, I realized that I like to be acknowledged but, being fourth of six children, I was overlooked. Being among the middle children had its perks. I was not under the microscope and could test limits unlike my first and second siblings who were not afforded this luxury. But, when I craved the attention I had to jump through hoops to ensure I got what I needed. I envied not getting recognition just because of my birth order. In the trenches of the middle I needed to work on my uniqueness which ended up being the ability to connect and mediate at a young age. In vying for my positioning, I learned my unique skills quite early.

Think of your early Leadership experiences. The way that you need to be appreciated might impact how you view others' desire and method of acknowledgment. These pieces of awareness become vital as you develop your model for rewards and recognition.

## AUTHENTIC REFLECTING

What were some of the events and conditions that may have impacted your capacity to understand the role of recognition in your life?

What do you need to feel appreciated?

Do you need verbal approval? Or are you the type that gains acceptance based on your achievements?

How do you think of others who need acknowledgment in a different way from you?

Leading and the way you want to be recognized is the beginning point, but at that point you need to explore how other people want to feel when they are recognized. There are some willing to work away arduously without the recognition, believing that they are not as important as the stars in the organization. But each and every one of us wants to be seen and that is why it is so vitally important to understand the fabric of your culture and start there.

### Showing Acknowledgment

Your team members have a life that they bring with them when they come into your organization. By showing that you live the values of your culture is key but past that what methods might you employ to showcase all the people of your organization, even if they may not be the stars. Again, recognizing in others that they are important, in whatever format you decide is appropriate, increases morale, passion and productivity in exponential ways.

There are many methods that you can reward others especially as we have to factor in the virtual workplace. Feedback from employees is the first piece of information that should be deciphered. Then, when thinking through your company's core values, what are the innovative ways that awards and rewards can be shown. And doing this more often than the annual or quarterly meetings is definitely necessary.

The pace of our world is getting swifter with each passing year so, too, does our need to keep employees connected. In this environment, recognition is key. Monthly newsletters are a way to highlight the accomplishments of the month. Try implementing a peer-feedback session at the end of each week. In this weekly roundup someone who worked with a colleague can give that person a shout out and employees can also share a win that they have had in their personal life. This is a win-win scenario.

On an ongoing basis employees are staying connected and giving positive feedback to each other. It is the perfect link of connection that managers could use to assess how people are doing generally. Weekly connection is key to understanding the pulse of an organization and when feedback is peer to peer it creates a space that is genuine and not contrived, as it might be when coming from management. The need to consistently connect is something that most of us need and most of us spend more time working than we do with our families, even if we are working virtually.

When leading your meetings ensure that you structure it so there is the ability to understand where people are at on an emotional level.

According to recognition expert Christopher Littlefield,[25] asking, "How are you?" will not garner the information needed to know how your team is managing. Asking a more pointed question on a Likert scale,[26] such as "How well are you doing with the skills you presently have at your job?" will garner better information to gauge the pulse of each person in the meeting. If an individual records a number that is a bit lower, it is important to note this and follow up at some point.

Changing the structure of your meeting to incorporate a team-building activity is another suggestion. Make it about connection and the recognition and rewards information for your program will produce itself.

## TASKS FOR AUTHENTICITY

Are you a better communicator at work or at home? If there is a difference, where and how are you better? Think about why.

What are some elements that make you a better communicator at home or work?

Are there times that you are more patient in either environment and, if so, why? What are some of the elements that you notice when you are in this space?

In your early narrative, what did you learn about communicating effectively in reference to home and work life?

Reflect on your early role models and think how they viewed the value of connection at home versus work.

## Chapter 9

# CASE STUDY: AUTHENTIC MENTOR

Jim was not the kind of boss that I would have picked to lead me as his personality was so different from my own. He was very analytical and I was intuitive. He looked at most things from a different angle, a space that I often found difficult to understand.

He was able to remain disentangled with the emotional trappings of leading staff and this was a skill I needed to master quickly as a new Leader. He exuded an evenness that I admired. He appeared to stay out of the fray while being able to make solid decisions to resolve high conflict situations. Jim was able to read conditions quickly and provide the necessary guidance needed to foster contemplation and growth in staff.

He was able to recognize my strengths as a new Leader and provide the guidance needed for skill enhancement. His warmth was definitely on the low side but that made for the levelness that he was able to achieve with staff and building of our teams.

One of the core lessons he taught me was that I needed to demonstrate the skills that I wanted to see in my team. As a new Leader I rolled up my sleeves and demonstrated the skills needed to create confidence in my team by showing my capacity. When challenged in this setting I was guided to keep demonstrating credibility while starting to assert my role as Leader.

This team had been together for ten years and most of them had been in the clinical field for a long time. I needed to demonstrate my Leadership capacity by leading from a place of strength. With Jim's guidance, I was able to effectively deal with their perception of me as a young Leader and began to create a space for the team. He challenged me to take control in meetings but always to do this from a kind space.

My team was not trusting and I bore the brunt of previous Leadership. My staff needed to know that they could trust me. This was difficult as a new Leader but what I found valuable was the tempo of this mentor's feedback. He rarely, if ever, got upset. He had a unique refrain that he repeated often, "It is all street theater. You just have to figure out what role you are playing." At the time I was not aware how powerful this statement would become in my growth.

As a younger Leader I got pricked and prodded by my staff but Jim's guidance made me realize that I needed to grow through my triggers. When I was activated I would spend time trying to understand what was being sparked in me and what my response was all about. I had achieved the schooling to become a psychotherapist, but my growth was needed in the area of managing people. And this ability had to escalate in a short period of time.

Jim's counseling allowed me to understand my Leadership story. Comprehending the triggering personalities and the most effective ways to address concerns was vital to my growth. I learned how to appreciate different points of views and started to learn to appreciate different perspectives, rather than perceiving my staff's reactions as a derailment of the process. I learned to understand my internal landscape and that my team's reactions were valid based on their past Leadership experiences. I realized that the team needed to experience my trustworthiness. Trust is not like a light bulb. You cannot turn it on and off. I needed to make my staff feel safe and secure and my mentor held the space to allow my growth through this process as a Leader.

These Leadership lessons are ones that I have continued to utilize throughout my career. The beginning of my understanding of my Leadership story started to unfold in this environment. One of my core fundamental beliefs was that everyone deserves respect and this is a face that I strived to achieve in each Leadership role that I played throughout my career. My mentor created the space for my Leadership to grow at a very early stage of my career.

### Self-Awareness

- Leader provided space for mentorship
- He used his space of kindness along with firmness to guide the space for growth
- Analysis of interaction with teams reviewed weekly
- Discussion of ideal Leadership style
- Strategic discussion of each team member
- Discussion of elements needed for cohesion in team

### Balanced Processing

- Discussion of difficult scenarios with team
- Offering perspective on various aspects of team
- Overall review of business metrics and outcome expected of each team member and approach

### Relational Transparency

- Discussions of developing trust on team
- Historical situations with previous Leader
- SWOT (Strengths, Weaknesses and Other Threats) analysis team members
- Strategy for developing trust with each team member

### Connection

- Strengths and limitations of Leadership style
- Stressors of team and positions
- Discussions of structure of meetings and expected outcomes

## Recognition

- General understanding of recognition style
- Understanding of each team member's recognition needs
- Developing recognition events (daily, weekly, monthly, annually)

# INCUBATING YOUR AUTHENTIC LEADERSHIP SPACE

As an Authentic Heart Leader you have worked through a lot of things that would make you stretch as a person. The process of looking at oneself through a transparent lens takes a great deal of courage.

In making the choice to pick up this book and work the entire way through it shows the kind of Leader that you want to be. It is like a cycle of metamorphosis – from the pupa to the butterfly. It can be painful but the end result is beautiful.

It is going from a space of unknowing to knowing. Once you take this journey you cannot go backwards.

*Self-awareness* is a gift that you give to yourself as a Leader, and incidental benefits come along with this process. *Balanced processing* provides a checkpoint to ensure you have the proper checks and balances in decision making. *Relational transparency* delivers the gift of understanding how your internal space is a reflection of how others relate to you. *Connection* ensures your mirror neurons are in sync with those you touch. *Recognition* allows you to remember always that all humas have a fundamental need to be seen and valued. With self-awareness comes a reality that all is possible and you are able to create an aerial view of what is needed for each and every element of your space. It starts with the Leader and ends with the Leader's space of connectivity.

This transformation will create a different intensity of connection in each and every aspect in your life. Your teams will enjoy the benefit of feeling seen and heard on a deeper level, which affords a certain degree of productivity that, by conventional standards, would not be otherwise possible. That deep place will allow all systems in your life to have the ultimate space that is sincerely possible in you as a Leader but also as a person.

The concept of linear thinking has long been a thing of the past but the post-pandemic environment will take the concept of VUCA (Volatility, Uncertainty, Complexity and Ambiguousness)[27] to a whole new level.

During a pandemic, like the COVID-19 event in 2020-22, or any other crisis, we learn that we can make changes rapidly. A lot of environments will adapt in such a way that efficiencies may be created that, in another time, would not be realized. What do we learn about ourselves as people, as Leaders and as teams during and after a crisis?

With the COVID-19 pandemic, we learned that globally we needed to be better prepared for bigger issues that can bring the world to its knees. We learned that our need for connection is key and have adapted our connection to others by having zoom family calls and drive-by birthday parties. As a world we became more aware of the importance of our space because we were forced to slow down and become more conscious.

While crises can be traumatic and tragic, if you dig beneath that you will find some positives too. In order to make this continuing transformation, you need to stay conscious as a Leader. Each and every one of you need to continue to play a Leadership role in your lives as a critical situation or a pandemic can gift you an opportunity to create better spaces both at home and at work.

Your heart is the sign post that gives your body all the information that tells you that you are on the right path. When you are connected to your heart, everything falls into place. You are able to stay in line with what you value and from that space comes all the things that are needed for optimal Leadership. The bumps along the way of life are reviewed and cleared, freeing up the path for your Authentic Leadership Legacy.

My Leadership legacy was to allow all around me to have a voice. This started from a little space in me that was borne out of my life circumstances. Your Leadership legacy should be clearly mapped out after doing the work. Leaving your mark is something that most Leaders want in their tenure. Reflecting on the steps that you will take from this point onwards should be fairly evident. However, this process will take place till the end of your career. We change continually so it is vitally important that we use all the tools to stay fluid in our shifts.

True Authentic Leadership is constant for the rest of your life as a Leader. I hope you keep the task to be the best version of who you are as a Leader at hand, current and focused. Leading from the heart will never steer you wrong with continued awareness.

# END NOTES

## Creating Space

[1] The term VUCA, which stands for Volatility, Uncertainty, Complexity and Ambiguousness, was created by the US Army War College based on writings from Warren Bennis and Burt Nanus, specifically *Leaders: The Strategies for Taking Charge*, 2nd ed. (Harper Business, 2012). Also see my podcast: https://roxannederhodge.com/creating-better-leaders-through-self-awareness/

## Chapter 1: TRUSTING AUTHENTIC CULTURE

[2] Clarine M. Jacobs, "Ineffective-Leader-Induced Occupational Stress" in SAGE Open (Volume 9, Issue 2, April-June 2019): https://doi.org/10.1177/2158244019855858. Also see my podcast: https://roxannederhodge.com/mental-health-in-the-workplace-with-bernie-dyme/

[3] *Ibid.* Also see my podcast: https://roxannederhodge.com/healthy-corporate-culture-with-hema-crockett/

[4] Catrina Kronfli, Senior Policy Analyst, Ontario Chamber of Commerce, "Mental Wellness in the Workplace: A Playbook for Employers" (May 2021). See: https://www2.deloitte.com/content/dam/Deloitte/ca/Documents/about-deloitte/ca-en-about-blueprint-for-workplace-mental-health-final-aoda.pdf. Also see my podcast: https://roxannederhodge.com/psychological-implications-for-returning-to-work-with-rensia-melles/

[5] CAMH, "Workplace Mental Health: A Review and Recommendations" (January 6, 2020). See: https://www.camh.ca/-/media/files/workplace-mental-health/workplacementalhealth-a-review-and-recommendations-pdf.pdf?la=en&hash=5B04D442283C004D0FF4A05E3662F39022268149. Also see my podcast: https://roxannederhodge.com/mental-health-part-2-with-bernie-dyme/

[6] Society for Human Resource Management, "Average Cost-per-Hire for Companies Is $4,129, SHRM Survey Finds" (Press Release: August 3, 2016). See: https://www.shrm.org/about-shrm/press-room/press-releases/pages/human-capital-benchmarking-report.aspx. Also see my podcast: https://roxannederhodge.com/motivating-teams-with-david-miles/

[7] Gracia Chua, "The True Cost of Hiring a New Employee in Canada" (Enkel Backoffice Solutions). See: https://www.enkel.ca/blog/bookkeeping/true-cost-

new-hire-canada/. Also see my podcast: https://roxannederhodge.com/authentic-leadership-through-recognition-with-sarah-mcvanel/

[8] Bill George, *Discover Your True North: Becoming an Authentic Leader*, expanded and updated edition (John Wiley & Sons, 2015). Also see my podcast: https://roxannederhodge.com/strategic-leading-through-an-authentic-lens/

[9] In their formative years, all leaders may be exposed to different perspectives or points of view on the world. When leaders are able to come to a heighted awareness of their point of view, then they are able to take into account all other perspectives and not become shortsighted. Based on their capacity to stay present and take each and every point of view in mind, leaders can make decisions that are best for the collective versus the narrow-minded few or the limited view of the senior leadership team. Also see my podcast: https://roxannederhodge.com/compassion-and-empathy-with-wade-thomas/

### Chapter 2: AUTHENTICITY QUOTIENT FOR LEADERSHIP

[10] Clement Bellet, Jan-Emmanuel De Neve, and George Ward, "Does Employee Happiness Have an Impact on Productivity?" (October 14, 2019). Saïd Business School WP 2019-13. Available at SSRN: https://ssrn.com/abstract=3470734 or http://dx.doi.org/10.2139/ssrn.3470734. Also see my podcast: https://roxannederhodge.com/achieve-a-state-of-flow-with-omer-aziz/

[11] Jade Scipioni, "Oprah Winfrey: After interviewing 37,000 people I learned everyone shares this 1 thing" (Feb 15, 2020) on CNBC.com. Also see my podcast: https://roxannederhodge.com/authentic-leadership-through-recognition-practices-part-ii-with-sarah-mcvanel/

### Chapter 3: THE HEARTBEAT MODEL

[12] Bill George, *Discover Your True North: Becoming an Authentic Leader*, expanded and updated edition (John Wiley & Sons, 2015). Also see my podcast: https://roxannederhodge.com/developing-leadership-skills/

### Chapter 4: SELF-AWARENESS

[13] Bill George, *Discover Your True North: Becoming an Authentic Leader*, expanded and updated edition (John Wiley & Sons, 2015). Also see my podcast: https://roxannederhodge.com/authentic-leadership-through-recognition-with-sarah-mcvanel/

14 Emma Young, "Lifting the Lid on the Unconscious" *New Scientist* in Humans, July 25, 2018. See: https://www.newscientist.com/article/mg23931880-400-lifting-the-lid-on-the-unconscious/. Also see my podcast: https://roxannederhodge.com/looking-at-the-shift-in-diversity-inclusion-today-with-tina-varughese/

15 "The Triune Brain" (Oct 26, 2016) at: https://www.thescienceofpsychotherapy.com/the-triune-brain/

16 American psychiatrist Aaron T. Beck laid the groundwork for the study of these distortions in the late 1960s, and his student David D. Burns continued research on the topic.

17 David D. Burns, *Feeling Good: The New Mood Therapy* (New York: Harper, 1980).

18 See "Employees Reveal How Stress Affects Their Jobs" (May 31, 2020) at: https://www.businessnewsdaily.com/2267-workplace-stress-health-epidemic-perventable-employee-assistance-programs.html#:~:text=Stress%20has%20been%20called%20the,%2C%20pervasive%20problem%2C%20experts%20say. Also see my podcast: https://roxannederhodge.com/authentic-living-with-roxanne-with-resiliency-expert-erika-caspersen/

## Chapter 6: **RELATIONAL TRANSPARENCY**

19 Also see my podcast: https://roxannederhodge.com/building-teams-that-make-great-things-happen-with-leadership-expert-yves-doucet/

## Chapter 7: **CONNECTION**

20 Published in the *Attachment and Loss* trilogy (1969, 1972 and 1980), Bowlby's theories continue to be studied. Also see my podcast: https://roxannederhodge.com/corporate-culture-with-mohammad-anwar/

21 A nonprofit organization, the HeartMath Institute's mission is to help people bring their physical, mental and emotional systems into balanced alignment with their heart's intuitive guidance. See: https://www.heartmath.org/

22 See Dr. Rollin McCraty, "Heart-Brain Coherence," Quantum University (November 2016) at: https://www.youtube.com/watch?v=MO3SGkI3B-I

23 Mac McCarthy, FSA, MAAA and Michelle Mudge-Riley, D.O., MHA, "Reformed Church in America – Analysis of HeartMath Experience" (November 2009) at: https://www.heartmath.org/research/research-library/organizational/reformed-church-in-america-d-analysis-of-heartmath-experience/

24 Rollin McCraty, PhD, Director of Research at the HeartMath Institute.

*Chapter 8:* **RECOGNITION**

[25] Christopher Littlefield is an International and TEDx Speaker specializing in employee appreciation, recognition, and workplace culture, and the founder of Beyond Thank You. See: https://beyondthankyou.com/. Also see my podcast: https://roxannederhodge.com/team-building-in-uncertain-times-with-christopher-littlefield/

[26] A Likert scale is a psychometric scale commonly involved in research that employs questionnaires and is the most widely used approach to scaling responses in survey research. The scale is named after its inventor, psychologist Rensis Likert.

## Incubating Your Authentic Leadership Space

[27] See footnote 1.

**ROR+**

Return on Relationships

HOW RETURN ON RELATIONSHIPS CAN IMPACT YOUR BOTTOM LINE

Keynote Speaker

Trainer

Author

Mental Health and
Wellness Expert

Registered Psychotherapist

Corporate Consultant

Podcaster Host

### KEYNOTES

Roxanne offers four
specialized keynotes that
can be customized to suit
your specific needs.

### WORKSHOPS

Roxanne's keynotes are
available as half-day or
full-day workshops.

### COACHING

Roxanne is available for
personalized leadership
for one-on-one or
group sessions.

CREATING THE SPACE FOR
**POSITIVE, HEALTHY CHANGE**
IN ORGANIZATIONS

**WEBSITE**
roxannederhodge.com

**EMAIL**
roxanne@roxannederhodge.com

**CHAT WITH ROXANNE**
chatwithroxanne.com

**LINKEDIN**
linkedin.com/in/roxannederhodge

**TWITTER**
twitter.com/roxannederhodge

**INSTAGRAM**
instagram.com/roxannederhodge